Domestic Aesthetic

JEAN BERNARD HEBEY

Domestic Aesthetic
Household Art 1920–1970

The Jean Bernard Hebey Collection
with the collaboration of Alain Ménard
Documentalist Jérémie l'Hostis

Photographs by Christophe Fillioux
with the assistance of Kihong Park

Translated by Ann McKeever

CONTINENTS

Art director
Fayçal Zaouali

Layout
Maria Letizia Lo Bosco

© 2002 - 5 Continents Editions srl, Milan
info@5continentseditions.com

ISBN 88-7439-017-3

Table of Contents

Acknowledgements

I should like to thank all my friends, family and colleagues who have accompanied me on this long, bizarre quest and who hardly ever doubted my intellectual faculties!

Gill Friesen, and Janet, for being the first to see nearly all these objects in his kitchen, when I came back exhausted from Californian Flea Markets and above all because Gill is "My brother".

Claude Deloffre, my childhood friend, for giving me hospitality during my countless stays in Los Angeles, because she shares my love of "beautiful images", because she is the epitome of elegance, and because she's the best "Godmother Claude" in the world!

Christian Ghion, her new husband, for his talent, although he's not dead yet!

Alain Ménard because he was the pioneer, guide, source and visionary who occasionally allowed me to share his "planet".

Eric Ghysels, because he's a man of many talents! His enthusiasm, tenacity, culture, taste and precision make him a publisher one would wish for anyone with a unique project. Without him this book would not have come about! Or at least not in this form! And Marco Jellinek, his alter ego at 5 Continents Editions, because he's living proof that it's possible to combine management and creativity and that being a "gentleman" is above all a state of mind. Fayçal Zaouali because he graced the layout with cosmopolitan elegance, both in front of and behind his computer.

Claude Cherki for his clear advice and patience.

Christophe Fillioux and Kihong Park for employing their many talents on my inanimate objects and for knowing how to show their "souls".

Isabelle Micale who for several years now has been sorting out all my insoluble problems connected with databases, bibliographies and eBay, but also for having shared my doubts and uncertainties …

Jérémie l'Hostis for having scoured the Internet in search of vital information which sometimes escaped my attention and for having pointed out objects that only he knew about!

Alain and Marie-Thérèse Perrin for their love of art and modernity, their two stunning chromed heaters from HMV (Vol. 2), their curiosity and their "eye". Also for their unpretentiousness, vibrancy, their Château La Grézette (the Wine as well as the Building) and their unfailing friendship over so many years.

Bernard Matussiére for his technicolor laughs and his black and white pictures.

Leslie Grunberg because he knows how to read texts, and men.

Claude Nobs for his Festival de Montreux, his extraordinary archives, his collections of juke-boxes and electric trains and his coffee-maker.

Daniel Filipacchi because I owe him so much! I am what I am because of him and I never get a chance to tell him.

Michael Leon and Leslie Dart for receiving several tons of packages and for having allowed me to cram them into their 5th Avenue cellar… very chic! But above all for being my friends!

Paola Antonelli for her smile, her time, her energy, her encouragements, her femininity and her curiosity… *Grazie, Bella*!

Axel Brucker, "The King of the Mac-Mahon, Trailers and Dinky Toys", for the countless hours he spent at the Paris Flea Market watching me haggle over Tupperware in the freezing cold ! ("I don't believe it!"). May the Great Pontiac be always with you!

Helena Pardo who for almost thirty years now has been watching over me, pampering me and looking after my objects, and who, without abandoning me, has grown to adore my daughters and my wife!

Jean-Pierre Buscat, arbiter of elegance, both textile and moral. The only person with whom I could go to the flea markets in the USA without fear of boredom, competitiveness or lack of culture! "Godfather Jean-Pierre", you're part of the family!

Malo de Lastelle for having understood and realized my computerized fantasies.

Barbara and Dorothy, my two Belgian sisters-in-law, for having so often allowed me to acquire, with Belgian francs, the weird objects that only family love could excuse!

Aimé Maeght and his Nicole for his "bargain hunting" eye, his generosity, his stories and passions.

Jacques Bonnaval of the Saint-Etienne Biennale, for having understood where I was going and for his kind-hearted tenacity.

Susan Ashbrook for being my long-time "Californian early bird", and for her strength and courage.

Lionel Bochurberg for knowing how to read and write between the lines.

Sylvain Papeloux for his kindness, his advice, both legal and personal, for putting up with my impatience and for sharing some of my ideas, particularly about the USA!

Eli Buck, the New York Pirate with the most amazing treasure imaginable! For the couple of hours that he always manages to find for me. I value your time!

Gianna Caratenuto for her enthusiasm, her natural kindness and because we all love you.

Alexander von Vegesack for enabling me to meet Eric Ghysels, because we've had an identical "bargain hunting" career and for having achieved the ultimate dream for collectors, the Vitra Design Museum.

Alexandre Mériel for having been my guide at Vitra in Weil am Rhein and for having allowed me to visit Ali Baba's cave.

Philippe Starck because he's so annoying for having understood it all!

Cameron Watson for his friendship, his love of France, and his hip English!

Bernard Lion for our Jazz and Flea Markets escapades in New York.

Florence Michel for her energy, her dad, her stylish skiing, her knowledge of design and her time.

Dominique Ilous for her "Insider's Trading" at Paul Bert.

Frédérique Hermé Grasser for having been the first, once again! And for having nourished me, body and soul, more often than I deserved! Thanks also to Pierre Hermé, the world's Best Pastry Chef... Thanks for those sweet, spicy, caustic, warm moments!

Alain Bernard for having smuggled several kilos of chrome from Los Angeles to Paris.

Pierre Hebey for making excuses—saying it's all due to family genes—for these strange passions.

Jean Fernandez (l'Aigle des Montagnes) for having made fun of me with so much humour that it was almost an encouragement (I miss you!).

But most of all to Renée, Lucille, Joséphine, and Laura Hebey, the women in my life, for having put up with, excused and sometimes even encouraged this collection.

For different reasons "I love you"!

Introduction

John Lennon didn't bat an eyelash, "The Empire State Building!"
His reply to the clichéd question—"What souvenir would you like to bring back to England from your USA tour?"—was not only brilliant but also conceptual, irreverent, threatening and witty!

Those four words said it all: fascination with the USA, appropriation of the most famous symbol of American power, glorification of the skyscraper myth, an inordinate appetite for the awesomely modern Art Deco architecture and the POPularisation of a "chromo". After conquering the hearts and pocket money of teenagers in the richest country in the world, why shouldn't a triumphant Beatle want to bring home the Empire State Building?

As a contemporary of Lennon's my answer and attitude, without missing a beat, would have been the same as his! The big difference between us was that I followed my fantasy through to its logical conclusion!

Bit by bit, right under the nose of French and American customs officers, I snuck back to France, maybe not the Empire State Building, but a great many of the objects which symbolize and encapsulate American aesthetic culture over the last fifty years.

It's tricky writing for a book devoted to photos of objects that make up what has been described as a "very special" collection and one so closely tied up with one person: me.

You either go for the impersonal approach, writing something that aims to intellectualize, give credibility, maybe even rationalize and justify what is, after all, just a harmless, if somewhat cumbersome, passion. And then you end up writing one of those pseudo-cultural studies, laced with a bit of history and criticism that you get at the beginning of every book on design you buy and which I make a point of skipping.

Or else, if you're more of a talker than a writer, you explain it all in the first person, using those famous journalistic who, when, why, where and what as well as the more mundane, how much.

As it's hard to be objective about my life as a collector, in view of the time and resources I've devoted to it for close on 40 years, I've naturally chosen the second solution, not from narcissism but more for the sake of simplicity.

My experiences, mistakes, hopes, tantrums and purchases over 40 years of bargain hunting, dedicated to objects that I've brought back from trips from far and near, have enabled me to get a deeper understanding and a better handle on places, times and eras.

This is obviously autobiographical, but also, I hope, historical. I want to try and share my enthusiasms but also some of what I have learned with the rare readers of this type of work who, unlike me, read the text first and then look at the (far more revealing) pictures.

Background

 Born in France, brought up in Paris, I'm part of a family, but also a generation, or at least a social category, that was raised against a backdrop of American culture (two words that nowadays tend to make the ignorant and blinkered smirk).

My parents listened to jazz: Basie, Ellington, Armstrong. They took me to the movies, to the Mac-Mahon or Cinéac Ternes, to see undubbed versions of westerns and musicals and they also spoke fluent English.

My mother adored Frank Sinatra, and wanted to look like Audrey and Katherine Hepburn (which she did).

My father worshipped Clark Gable (he had his mustache), Errol Flynn (he didn't have his physique) and Marilyn Monroe. The only thing he had in common with her was that Yves Montand was a pal of his! He loved *Les Puces* (the Paris Flea Market) and often took me there even when I was just a young kid.

I spent my vacations staying with families in England in order to learn English, I had Hopalong Cassidy and Roy Rogers cowboy boots, I casually wore the blue jeans that my dad brought back for me from the USA. I dreamed of being an American one day so that I could at long last be "in living color!"

Actually, for reasons now made clear (by the media), but which I didn't know at the time, up until the age of 15 in 1960, if I gave any thought at all to what was then known as the Soviet Union, the USSR or "The country behind the Iron Curtain", the images that came to mind were always black and white. Well, gray really! Likewise for Europe!

Gray images started to morph into pastel-colored postcards in places like England after "rock" singers such as Cliff Richard or Tommy Steele burst onto the scene. Italy and Spain have always enjoyed a privileged "in color" status, no doubt due to Vespas, the Costa Brava and because they held out the promise of vacations.

France stuck stubbornly to the color of its television with its single channel (broadcasting a full 4 hours a day) and its colorful (gray) presenters!

Whenever I thought of America, however, what came to mind was a riot of colors, sun, young women in bikinis, playing volleyball and eating Sunkist grapefruits. Night and day, pink automobiles would cruise silently along endless traffic-jam free highways with their bodywork shimmering each time they passed the neon lights of a gas station.

Even back then, I felt outrage and incomprehension at this blatant injustice!

Why did we all have to pile into a 4 CV or a Dauphine which were cute but ridiculously pokey, when an American Hebey family could lounge in a spacious Ford or a Pontiac Cruiser? And for the same price too.

Why did our tiny long-wave radio stations (a total of five for the whole of France) play only accordion music, when Elvis existed "over there" and thousands of radio stations were blasting out rock music 24 hours a day?

Why weren't we allowed to buy and wear Levis, button-down collar shirts, penny loafers, college sweaters, baseball jackets with their three-colored stripes, the basics, for heaven's sake?

Why was I, who was a bit too tall and a bit too big for my age, forced to wear pants that were too short or sleeves that barely reached my wrists when "over there", I was a normal 42 long?

Why did I have to listen to second-rate cover versions of hit records whereas "they" could have the original versions?

Why wasn't the school bus yellow?

Why was the American President (J. F. Kennedy) young and well-dressed (by Brook Brothers) with a pretty, young wife at his side while mine was an old soldier, wearing a general's uniform (De Gaulle) and married to a crabby school teacher?

Why did I still have to grind coffee by hand when the average American just had to push a button on an electric coffee maker?

Why was it that everything modern was either forbidden or inaccessible?

Why was I forced to be old, from a very early age, whereas "they" could be forever young?

This was my state of mind, as a sixteen year-old in 1961, when I took a propeller-driven plane to New York.

The Discovery of America

 It was just like the movies! Larger than life! The films didn't have French subtitles and the houses had 6-figure numbers. Everything matched the reality of *West Side Story* a movie I had seen 17 times!

After spending two days in New York, I took a bus to cross America, destination Los Angeles. It was a Greyhound bus, designed, of course—but I didn't know it then—by Raymond Loewy. Los Angeles seemed to mirror the silver screen: Sunset Boulevard, Santa Monica, Hollywood. They were all there! And in color too! With a warm, diffuse light just like the movies.

I had the feeling that everything had been thought out, designed, built to last or at least give that impression. There was no stinting on quantity or quality. Chrome, steel, metals in every form were used, without counting the cost. Welcome to the land of plenty.

One thing was clear: America was *Rich* and Europe was *Poor* !

In America, just about everything was made of metal: diner stools, sugar bowls and salad bowls, among others. Meanwhile, in Europe, the coffee grinders, kitchen utensils and dining room chairs were made out of wood—which has a charm all of its own! Today, forty years on and after reading so much on the subject, I have a better grasp of the historical, social and economic reasons behind that disparity and the overwhelming impression of wealth.

Short History of Industrial Design for Beginners

 Taking as a starting point this simple difference between raw materials (metal versus wood), it becomes easy to explain various factors concerning modern Industrial Design. For a start, metals are long-lasting and can withstand for years the kind of usage—washing, scratching, wear and tear—inherent to that type of object.

Wood, in contrast, decays, breaks, self-destructs. So, in the USA today, you find cooking utensils, from the 40's and 50's, still in perfect condition. The same can hardly be said about the wooden washboards, straw brooms and stoneware pots which belonged to our grandmothers!

Historically, there are many different reasons for this state of affairs:

Prior to their intervention in World War II, the huge American war effort meant that they needed to construct heavy industrial plants or convert existing ones. Between 1940 and 1945, America used forty per cent of its economic resources on its war needs. It invested twenty five billion dollars in new factories, new equipment and new developments in chemistry and computing. Once the war was over, all the surplus aluminium, steel and metal had to be put to use.

The decision was soon made, and swiftly implemented, to make automobile fenders instead of airplane wings and milkshake mixers instead of bombs. Structurally, the US economy has a duty to produce, this is its role, its vocation, its mission. The only way to supply nearly sixty million homes with instruments of progress was by making use of industry and homogeneous assembly line production.

Europe with its menders of pots and pans was already lagging way behind!

As for automobiles, in order to achieve cheap mass-production, upstream planning was vital, machines had to take the place of humans, and the object had to be machine-made from A to Z. Human intervention was only needed for quality control or for monitoring machines.

Added to this, the USA saw a significant rise in purchasing power, the end of mass immigration which had tended to favor mechanization, the development of electricity and a boom in the construction industry. To crown it all, Fordism and Taylorism had succeeded in rationalizing, standardizing and managing work scientifically.

Over twenty or so years, all of these factors, combined with an exponential economic upturn, fuelled by a more efficient supply of cheap electricity would lead to the democratization of new "home helps" such as the refrigerator.

From now on, both *middle class* and *working class housewives* would use the same objects! One side-effect of all this: the (temporary) disappearance of cleaning ladies!

Rampant capitalist industry had dealt the class struggle a cruel blow!

The revolution had taken place without Europe knowing it!

Because of industrialization, it was no longer the *master craftsman* who served the *client*, whether church, state or middle classe, a client whose role it was to *commission* an object according to his desires, needs or tastes, and who also imposed his own *good taste*.

From now on, it would be a *technician* who would design—designate an object which would be produced on an industrial scale and sold to a mass market. Thus, the most singular feature of Industrial Design would become apparent. The human hand need play no part in its manufacture.

Finally, it's worth noting that, paradoxically, a common aim of what is known generically as "Industrial Design" is to conceal the actual industrial elements, wires, gear wheels, pistons, etc., which form the essential workings or "guts" of the machine.

This Industrial Revolution enabled man to progress from using technical skills, developed over the years, know-how and dexterity, to merely *conceptualizing* an idea, a *form*, a *function* and then implementing it with the aid of *industry*.

This new industrial era would demystify manufactured products and allow *mass production* and a *mass aesthetic*. This was naturally derided by the middle classes because they now faced the horrible prospect that all and sundry would now have access to the best same quality.

By allowing this shift from craftsmanship to industry, from the elite to the masses, Industrial Design grew in status, no longer content with an artistic veneer, preferring to see itself as an *industrial product*. Design would demand the creation of *originals*, instead of *copies*.

This approach would be taken to new heights from the 1950's onwards with the birth of the *"disc record"*. In fact, there is no original of a disc record. Everyone owns the original. This is the first real application of the idea of *"multiple"*.

What's more, it's this very notion of "non-uniqueness" which would pose so many problems for museum curators in the future.

After World War I, the United States, helped by a talented wave of European immigrants, essentially designers from the German Bauhaus, decided to kick-start the economy with consumerism. To achieve this, the available products had to be made more appealing, more indispensable and above all "sexier"! Design, embodying a lifestyle concept, was the ideal and timely tool for this. It had to satisfy not only needs but also desires and it would be required on a massive scale!

Lurell Guild, Harold van Doren, Raymond Loewy, Henry Dreyfuss, John Vasos, Walter Downig Teague, Norman Bel Geddes, Russel Wright, were some of the names of the best known designers who were put to work. The coming together of the idealistic and utopian-minded European designers and the more pragmatic and commercially-minded Americans made for a winning combination!

"An object must fulfill its function perfectly: be practical, durable, cheap and beautiful", declared Walter Gropius, completely at ease with his status as designer for the masses.

America had the necessary raw materials, industrialization, mass production and mechanization to go into battle. The *hardware* was ready and now the *software* had to be fine-tuned to sell this production. Applying the lessons learned in Hollywood, industry would use and abuse the increasingly influential media: newspapers, radio, movies, gramophone records, automobiles, television. Everything was put to work in order to sell!

Marketing, merchandising and sales forces were boosted by this new miracle recipe: advertising which featured "The American Dream"!

From now on, *clients* would become *consumers*. They can, *must*, buy consumer goods on a regular basis. Thanks to this public-spirited action, they provide society with the means to pay them a salary, allowing them to consume once more. The wheel has come full circle. You have to consume to live and live to consume.

In the pragmatic and cynical words of Alfred P. Sloan, former Chairman of General Motors, industry invented perpetual movement by means of "planned obsolescence". The consumer society had arrived! Long live cheap, attractive, self-destructing and disposable mass production!

While all this was going on, Europe was still crazy about craftsmanship, localised production, as well as that celebrated but debilitating "dexterity".

California

 At 16, I was oblivious to all these social, economic, historical and philosophical considerations. On the one hand, you had "the old folk" with their traditions who had lost the war with their compromises and concessions. And on the other, you had the "fun-loving", modern, open-minded "youngsters" who had won the war. Although I didn't know it, I "felt" that they would win the next one, the economic war!

For the time being, all I cared about were the streamlined cars, strawberry-colored radios, tanned surf boards, and best of all, was the sheer profusion and availability of it all. The stores were packed full of everything! In every size, in every material, in every color, for every taste! Even though I hadn't lived through the war and never had to endure post-war restrictions, when I was growing up in France, all I ever seemed to hear was a tetchy, "No, there isn't any !" In America, it was just the opposite. "Yeah! You bet we've got it!"

And lots of it too! You just had to be able to afford it and if it was beyond your means, all you had to do was take out a loan! (A taboo word in France until as late as the1970's.)

My new-found enthusiasm blinded me to the long term consequences of this world, which was not yet known as the *consumer society*.

For the time being, carried away with all this modernity, I stuffed myself with America. Let's face it, a country that owns an ice cream chain called "31 flavours" (Baskin & Robbins) can't be all bad! Especially when in Europe we had the choice between chocolate, coffee, vanilla and if you were very lucky, strawberry. Period! Don't even think about marshmallow!

Thousands of radio stations, hundreds of TV stations, highways criss-crossing the country (the only highway in France at that time was the 40 km-long "Autoroute de l'Ouest"), gas stations open night and day, the possibility of doing your shopping in supermarkets at midnight and on Sundays (still illegal in France), launderettes open to all, stores with permanent sales (also still illegal in France). All this just went to prove that this really was a land of milk and honey!

However, one thing should have struck me. What became of all these products? Where did they end up? In which cemeteries of modernity did they end their ephemeral lives? The answer would change my life. Or at least the amount of living space my life would now require!

Flea Markets - "Les marchés aux puces"

 The land of *more*, which was not yet the land of *too much*, fervently believed in the redemptive powers of *possession* and *happiness* through *consumption*. Natural resources and material goods were apparently inexhaustible!

In 1960, even though George Lucas's movie *American Graffiti* had yet to be released, for young Europeans, the 50's were a mythical period in which we had *existed*, but which we hadn't actually *experienced*. We were only 10 to 15 years old at the time.

It was time to catch up! We wanted the chrome-plated milkshake mixers, the jukebox-convertibles (Raymond Loewy), portable transistors, drive-in burgers with their roller-skating car hops. And if it was no longer possible to experience them in everyday life (apart from a few places that were my haunts for over 30 years until they finally died out) surely, you could at least buy these cult objects!

Taking up my Parisian bargain hunting habits again, on the second Sunday of the month, I was all set for action in Pasadena for the Rose Bowl. In contrast to French flea markets, in particular, and generally those in Europe which typically displayed objects, furniture, trinkets and so forth, were all at least 100 years old, and usually dated back one, two, or three centuries or even more, American flea markets were packed full of objects that were less than fifty years old!

Everything was modern, apart from the few erudite vendors with their displays of ornate antique tables or lamps (generally from Europe) which were over-embellished with copper. You could also find wonderful Native American objects (rugs, baskets, jewels, headdresses) vestiges of a violent but recent past. For the most part, however, the objects dated from the 30's 40's or 50's.

Flea markets are above all a ritual. You go there, preferably alone, rarely with a definite goal in mind. You don't go to *search* but to *find*. It's not about going after a precise object but rather about being open to any offer, any find.

The proverb, "curiosity killed the cat" does not apply to a flea market where you have to be curious about everything! All your senses need to be on a state of alert, you have to pay attention to a particular form, material, history, usage or technique. Your memory is also vital because it will tell you if you own it already, if you've already seen it, if you know "the thing"!

Your senses are really put to work in order to *see* something sticking out, *feel* an edge of a fabric or an old piece of paper, *listen to* the crackling of old leather, the tinkling of crystal or *touch* to distinguish between marble and alabaster, bronze or Babbitt metal. But though I have yet to see anybody *taste* an object, isn't taste the sum total of all the other senses where flea markests are concerned?

If the senses are important then memory and culture are too!

Vendors are the socio-professional group which has the greatest hunger for knowledge of them all. They consider documentary evidence as being the vital source for their activity and prosperity. It is generally acquired and consulted in the form of books, newspapers, magazines and publicity leaflets. Added to that, you have cinema, television, record sleeves, advertising (in the press, stuck on walls or shown at the cinema or on TV), newspaper and magazine covers or film posters—contemporary popular culture, basically.

Knowledge is what makes the difference: knowing that this seemingly uninteresting coffee maker, was designed by Henry Dreyfuss, that this sewing machine is by Nizzoli, that it was before such and such a year, that the production of this object was original with the designer having overall control and that after such and such a year, the marketing was taken over by a certain distributor who changed the diameter of the tube or the thickness of the metal. And so it goes on. Once again, knowledge is the determining factor.

The relationship between a collector and an object is almost family-like in nature. In the collection that I'm interested in, the object has virtually no intrinsic value. Its added value is what I give it by virtue of the fact that I have chosen it (the father) and also because it is linked to other objects which have also been chosen. Its value stems from being part of a set, which has much more value than the sum of its parts (family).

Nostalgia is closely bound up with flea markets. Inveterate bargain hunters devote themselves to what amounts to an induction course into the culture, lifestyles, customs and usages of a country.

Bargain hunting allows and encourages you to see, touch and maybe even possess objects, furniture, jewels, books which you had thought were long-vanished or unobtainable.

The desire for *originality* is a factor that shouldn't be underestimated: that feeling of being different from other people because you *dare* to live surrounded by second-hand furniture, sit in an armchair that once belonged to someone else or sleep in a bed that someone may have died in!

And finally, *money* is an essential element too in the game of acquiring objects. Knowing how much "that" is worth, how much you're prepared to pay, what added value will this object bring to the collection as a whole? What condition is it in and can it be restored and if so, how much will it cost? Is it more or much more than you can afford, or do you actually want it that much anyway? Your rapport with vendors, the occasional feeling that you've been ripped off or been extravagant, that you've bought a useless object or one that isn't particularly beautiful; it's all a bit of an ego test really. You need a lot of self-confidence to proudly carry home what a lot of people would consider only "fit for the trash can"!

A Vocation

It's not an easy task to rationalize, explain and analyze what at the time was merely a desire, a need to acquire what, for us we Europeans, was unobtainable! Deprived of modernity, I wanted to get to know and acquire every symbol of *progress*. A striking difference between Europe and the USA was this sensation of wealth through possession. This didn't imply that poverty didn't exist. Let's just say that in the USA, families of modest means seemed to be better off than rich families were in Europe!

Our cultures are defined, just as they were for the Egyptians, the Venetians or cavemen, by *objects*. They show how we live, what we eat, how we evolve in the world in which we work. These objects help us to find solutions to our problems and also explain how we communicate.

Just like a researcher at National Geographic or the CNRS (Centre for National Research in France) who feverishly searches for the plates, wood, bowls, spoons or clothes of our ancestors, the Gauls, Mayas or Africans, I had unconsciously decided to seek out and accumulate the vestiges of our contemporaries' lives. Tracking down, researching, bringing material proof which relates our history, bears witness to our invention and energy was now to be my mission in life. I had discovered my El Dorado, my Ali Baba's cave, where I would be the only thief. I would be an "archaeologist of modernity"!

The Rose Bowl and Pasadena City College, Veteran Stadium, Long Beach, the countless Thrift Stores of Los Angeles, Burbank, Glendale, Ventura, etc. on the West Coast, or Brimfield, the market on 26th and 6th in New York or the bi-annual Pier Show on the East Coast of the USA, would be my excavations sites for the next 30 years. My aim: find mythical objects which typified everyday life and, by extension, *progress*. I would exclude anything trivial: different representations of Mickey Mouse, Coca Cola objects, enamel advertising signs. Basically, anything that hadn't been "graced by the celestial hand of Industrial Design for the betterment of mankind". I would favor anything which had served everyday life... Discreetly but efficiently... And I'd make houseware my priority.

Desire and Necessity

Why tire yourself out doing something yourself when a machine can do it for you? Particularly as industrialization and, above all, the miniaturization of electricity now made it possible to manufacture *robots* (science fiction and its futuristic discourse play a key role in houseware) which, in their turn, were going to help bring about women's lib, long before the slogan was even conceived.

What originally drove design was quite simply the need to stretch our physical capacities. You write better with a pencil than you do writing with a finger on a wall, you go further and quicker with a bicycle than on foot, you drink better with a glass than with your hands, etc.

The word design comes from the word draw in Italian, *disegno,* which since the Renaissance has meant a plan, a drawing, a job to be carried out. This plan has to help create an object or service which will later be manufactured industrially. A bit of history!

Although houseware usually brings to mind the kitchen, it embraces the bathroom too. These two essential rooms in a home are *private places* that tend to be associated with women. All advertising for new objects to be used in these places focuses on women as well as the efficiency of the objects themselves. The reason for this is simple: the places of expression/display for these functional objects are the kitchen or bathroom, private places; in complete contrast to the "living areas" and *public places* where the fine arts flourish: furniture, paintings, rugs, china. It's no longer about *appearing* but *doing*.

What's more, these objects needed to be easy to clean as they were to be used in sanctuaries dedicated to hygiene. They therefore had to be able to be treatable by other (washing) machines. These were the constraints that would influence the choice of material which also had to be cheap. Ever-pragmatic and efficient, industry would use its powers of persuasion to target women

Domestic design was to undergo two diametrically opposed influences. One was objective, the result of new techniques or technologies, new materials and new tools which were more *scientific* or economic in origin. The other, totally subjective, had its origins in *the current climate*. Industrial design, therefore, needed to be useful, practical, efficient and cheap but would also have to conform to the prevailing idea of what was beautiful, fashionable (we didn't say hip in those days), and above all *modern*. All highly ephemeral notions and extremely beneficial to industry, which depends on constant renewal for its very survival.

The genius of design is that it is constantly at the crossroads of both of these seemingly paradoxical imperatives: *need* and *desire*

The kitchen and bathroom are the two places (temples) dedicated to the cult of the body. The kitchen is for storing, preparing and often consuming the food which has the most vital function of all of feeding us. These actions are generally carried out as a family.

The bathroom is for washing, grooming, getting ready and dressed. These actions are generally carried out alone. So it was going to take considerable tact, psychology, finesse (known as marketing these days) to be able to invade the nation's privacy!

The end result of all these constraints is paradoxical! In the name of women's lib, the system would use magazines, radio, movies and TV to sell an image of a woman which was efficient, modern and flattering. All she would have had to do to be exceptional would be to conform to this image and buy the products that matched the latest "kit"!

A further paradox is apparent when you compare the genuine liberation of the kitchen to the continued slavery in the bathroom! You must have this particular haircut, you need that beauty cream, this hair dryer is essential, this toothpaste, that slimming cream is necessary, and so on. Designers are faced with this duality on a daily basis. They have to dream up and produce essential or trivial objects, by responding to, or totally inventing, *urgent needs*.

Function and Decoration

 Since the first toaster came along, there hasn't been anything very new to say: You put the bread in, you turn on the toaster, you wait a bit and the bread is toasted!

It has a simple function which doesn't leave much room for creativity. It will take boundless ingenuity on the part of industry and designers to make us believe, year after year, that we must have the latest model!

Simple or double, with or without a timer, large enough to take a *baguette* (in France), with tongs to make *panini* (in Italy), one that grills on one side only (for the English), big enough to take 4 slices for big families. In 100 years of existence, the technical innovations have been minor to say the least!

But it's not for want of trying! There's the "Toastolator" which lets you see the progress of the toast during its grilling process, the pop-up which makes the slices, well, pop up; the one that spins the slices of bread like Chaplinesque ballerinas and the one that makes the slices drop instead of popping up, to mention a few.

Basically, nothing very earth shattering!

And yet, how many sleepless nights, tense board meetings, jobs on the line, broken marriages must have been brought about by a two-speed toaster! Not to mention the stock prices, economic indexes, market share all hinging on a wretched, variably grilled slice of toast. What's more, this phenomenon is perpetuated and requires even greater ingenuity today thanks to globalization. The ultimate dream is soon to come true. The same toaster from Beijing to Marseilles, from Miami to Vladivostok! Just imagine the consequences for industry, the stock market and politics!

As the *function* is always fundamental and unvarying, what would change through different eras and times was packaging and presentation, the skin, *make-up* and the powerful notion that consumers would project their own lives in acquiring this object.

In order to woo, and thereby persuade, you need to give an object, which is, after all, primary, an environment which expresses modernity, efficiency, self-confidence, and a belief in a better world. And all that with just a stroke of a pencil and a few aesthetic modifications!

Industrial designers, both famous and anonymous, but all serving industry, successively helped define the theme of modernity which stamped an era.

From 1925 to 1935, the symbols of the moment were skyscrapers. This would give us *step* styling, these buildings' trademark.

From 1935 to 1945, *streamline* styling was all the rage. Speed, futurism, internationalism and aero-dynamism.

From 1945 to 1955, it was the turn of *taper* styling, inspired by the streamlined automobiles which were the very essence of modernity.

From 1955 to 1965, this gave way to *sheer* styling, no doubt because it was tinged with geometric modernism.

Finally, in 1965, it was *sculpture* styling that dominated. Ill-digested modern art could sometimes wreak havoc!

Subsequently, it became harder to pinpoint and classify styles because Europe went straight from wood to plastic and began to beat the USA at its own game.

One can, however, distinguish several marked international trends: The 80's, like the stock market and computing, strived to be precise, efficient and robust. Everything was black, chrome-plated, with maybe just a touch of red.

In the 90's, cocooning produced a rounded, anamorphic style, one that was turned in on itself, well suited to the comfort of marriage, which was booming at the time and bringing up kids (a direct result of the previous act). The doubts and uncertainties of the early 21st century would find refuge in nostalgia for the forms of the 50's. With the exception of a few free spirits such as Marc Newson, Karim Rashid or Philippe Starck who continue, unashamedly, to express bold modernity.

Until 1970, all these trends allowed American industry to survive, prosper and produce all those objects with very simple primary functions and myriad designs.

The first object I brought back from my first trip to the USA was a Rival branded chrome-plated juicer. Its rounded, heavy form with a top which opened like a knight's helmet over a set of carnivorous, menacing teeth, made this the ultimate American object for me: powerful, robust, efficient and heavy! In Europe, a lemon squeezer consisted of a glass bowl, made of plastic if you were lucky, the only embellishment being its ridged, lemon-shaped centre. You would think that Europe hadn't yet discovered Archimede's principle! All the effort came from the force of the arm and the turn of the wrist.

That's how I began my collection which today comprises over 3,000 objects, mainly from the USA but also from Europe and a few from all over the world.

Collection - State - Museums

 Art and Commerce. These two seemingly paradoxical notions, lying at the very foundation of Industrial Design, have always struggled to find acceptance and be assimilated by European museums.

This, despite the fact that over the last five years or so, Industrial Design has become a subject which fascinates all social classes and for different reasons; industrialists in search of a new market, young people trying to furnish their homes cheaply, a hip designer looking for direction, politicians hungry for modernity or academics researching into the origins of our everyday life.

This passion is always glorified with the sometimes highly flexible notion of *art*.

Architecture, interior decoration, fashion and by association, textile, cars, and of course furniture all receive endless attention. They all are highly coveted and spark endless infighting.

All these disciplines belong to the *fine arts*. They bestow a cultural aura on all those involved in this field. Or at least that's what they think! When discussing Industrial Design decency always dictates finding artistic pretexts for doing so. Very few are brave enough to talk about the trivialities of houseware; washing dishes, drying hair, vacuuming and dusting, are not seen as noble tasks.

In 1990, the Museum of Modern Art in New York put on an exhibition with a provocative and alluring title: "High and Low". The whole point of this exhibition was to show that the 20th century had generated new art forms and it was time the public, museums and critics saw them for what they really were: a new expression, using the resources, techniques, media and channels put at its disposal in an era which was undergoing massive changes. Comic strips, videos, graffiti and, of course, design comprised the core of this exhibition. This hugely successful exhibition acted as a revelation which shook up pre-conceptions and created a new order. The fuss was all the greater, coming as it did from that most respectable and well-respected institution of Modern Art, the MoMA.

Despite this definitive exhibition, even today, traditional curators cannot bring themselves to display a washing machine, coffee maker or lemon squeezer! They have to give credibility to these "*common/private*" objects, embellish them, dress them up and drown them in a pseudo-artistic mish-mash, a mixture of "*noble/public*" painting, sculpture and furniture.

As if they somehow needed to find a cultural pretext, preferably validated by financial certitudes so as to create a credible environment, before accepting the idea of publicly displaying an object, produced in thousands/ millions of copies and sold cheaply to people in suburban temples of consumption.

This is particularly true in France which is normally eager to create state institutions. As with photography (which also combines commerce, industry and art), the French state has little involvement in the field of Industrial Design with the exception of what was the

CCI and a few individual initiatives. A point of convergence between art, fashion, industry, trends, distribution, technique and technology, Industrial Design has to be able to master globalization, manufacturing and communication and fit perfectly with its time.

All these reasons, no doubt, explain why France finds it so hard to flourish in a modern industrial context.

For the last 50 years, the USA, England, Germany, Switzerland, Belgium, Holland and even Russia have had state or semi-state institutions, devoted to promoting, assisting and supporting design such as the Bauhaus-Archiv Museum of Design, Vhutemas, Rat für Formgebung, the MoMA, the Pasadena Design Center, the Cooper-Hewitt National Design Museum, to name but a few.

Whereas France, which has the biggest number of museums per capita in the world, still has no National Design Museum.

It is also significant to note that the Vitra Design Museum, one of the world's most prestigious museums dedicated to design (mainly furniture), which each year organizes one or two major exhibitions on this theme with 10 exhibitions permanently circulating in museums throughout Europe and the rest of the world, has never managed in 10 years of existence to show even one of its exhibitions in France! This can no longer be put down to chance but to choice! Why should it be necessary to go abroad if we want to see what's happening in Industrial Design? Could we be reverting to the Fifties when, in this area at least, France was deprived of modernity? Must we once again leave our own country and visit foreign museums in order to see one of the disciplines in which we excel!

As regards Industrial Design from 1950 to 1970, for the first time in the history of taste, it was Europe that looked towards the USA for inspiration. However, by applying a golden rule of their system, "If it ain't broke, don't fix it!", the Americans have lost sight of the original reasons behind the success of their production: dreams, fashion and desire. Nowadays, they are only interested in necessity. As a result, they're churning out the same toaster today they made 20 years ago!

Since 1970, the situation has reversed. Europe in general and France in particular, with Philippe Starck, are rapidly overtaking America when it comes to Industrial Design.

European industrialists have been shrewd enough to seize their chance. Captains of industry have commissioned gifted designers to dream up and design everyday objects which are practical, sometimes cheap and beautiful. Alessi, Habitat, Target, but also SEB, Moulinex, Braun, Calor and Philips produce hundreds of designed objects every year.

It is high time to pay a glowing tribute to the thousands of anonymous designers who, day after day, produce houseware utensils whose art galleries are called Darty, Fnac, Target or Safeway.

This collection was originally driven by adolescent frustrations.

Today, as a systematic collector and very much an adult, I wanted to show just how beautiful these objects really were and to demonstrate that you only have to open your eyes to see just how fascinating our environment can be!

Like Andy Warhol who, by "Showing" cans of Campbell Soup or packages of Brillo Pads, turned them into works of art, I simply wanted to "Show" that we all have treasures in our home and that we should "See" them now rather than wait for them to be glorified by nostalgia.

After 30 years of acquisition, I ended up learning a thing or two about these objects and my passion for them.

The Function... Whether it sucks up, turns, squeezes, heats, ventilates, cuts, burns, irons or blows is somewhat primary.

The Material... is important, but secondary.

What really counts is... *The Form!*

How this shape manages to express the longings, fears, desires and fashions, in other words, the *modernity* of an era.

Inevitably modern, these shapes have often been victims of fashions, trends, fads and mannerism. But they are also the realization of man's progress, technique, invention, hopes and aspirations. These objects are objective testaments to our frequent failures and occasional triumphs!

Jean Bernard Hebey

Bibliography

We have only cited a limited number of references, mainly for works of general interest. We have not cited monographs, magazines or websites. Listing these different sources could fill a book on their own.
I should like to thank all the authors who have enabled me to analyse and gain a deeper understanding of these objects, their sources, backgrounds and their place in history. I must certainly have been unintentionally "inspired" by all the material I have read over thirty years. I certainly wouldn't claim to have gained all this knowledge *ex-nihilo*. I simply compiled a certain number of widely held ideas which, over time, I ended up making my own!

8e Biennale Intérieur 82, biennale internationale de la créativité dans l'Habitat (Courtrai, 16-24 oct. 1982). Courtrai: 1982.

20th Century Design in Europe and America Selections from the Collection of the Museum of Modern Art, New York. Exhibition catalogue (Tokyo, The National Museum of Modern Art, 1957). Tokyo: The National Museum of Art, 1957.

Abadie, D., P. Arbaizar and L. Bayle. *Les Années 50*. Exhibition catalogue (Paris, Centre Georges Pompidou, 30 june-17 oct. 1988). Paris: Centre Georges Pompidou, 1988.

Aldersey, W. H. *New American Design: Products and Graphics for a Post-Industrial Age*. New York: Rizzoli, 1988.

Ambasz, E. *Italy: The New Domestic Landscape, Achievements and Problems of Italian Design*. Exhibition catalogue (New York, The Musem of Modern Art, may-sept. 1972). New York: The Museum of Modern Art, 1972.

Amic, Y. *Intérieurs. Le Mobilier français 1945-1964*. Paris: Ed. du Regard, 1983.

Anargyros, S. *Intérieurs. Le Mobilier français 1980*. Paris: Ed. du Regard, 1983.

Antonelli, P. *Workspheres: Design and Contemporary Work Styles*. Exibition catalogue (New York, The Museum of Modern Art, 8 feb.-22 apr. 2001). New York: The Museum of Modern Art/Harry N. Abrams, 2001.

Art in Progress: A Survey Prepared for the Fifteenth Anniversary of The Museum of Modern Art, New York. Exhibition catalogue (New York, The Museum of Modern Art, 1944). New York: The Museum of Modern Art, 1944.

Bangert, A. *Der Stile der 50er Jahre: Mobel und Ambiente*. München: Heyne, 1983.

——. *Der Stile der 50er Jahre II: Design und Kunsthandwerk*. München: Heyne, 1983.

Barré-Despond, A. *L'Union des Artistes Modernes*. Photograps by J.-B. Rouault. Paris: Ed. du Regard, 1986.

Battersby, M. *The Decoratives Twenties*. London: Studio Vista, 1976

Bayley, S. *In Good Shape: Style in Industrial Products 1900 to 1960*. New York: Van Nostrand Reinhold, 1979.

Bernadotte, S. *Industrial Design*, Göteborg: Wezatas Schriftserie 6, 1953.

Berkowith, R. A., J. A. McMaster, and D. A. Taragin. *The Alliance Of Art and Industry: Toledo Designs for a Modern America*. New York: Hudson Hills Press, 2002.

Besacier, H., B. Marcade, G. Monnier, P. Restany, and J. Rouzaud. *Catalogue d'exposition de la quadriennale internationale de Design: Caravelles* (Grenoble, Lyon, Saint-Etienne 22 june-25 sept. 1986). Grenoble: Studio Totem/Florence Philip and Jacques Bonnot, 1986.

Betsky, A., S. Flusty, J. R Lane, D. E. Nye, and C. Pearlmann. *Icons: Magnets of Meaning*. San Francisco: Betsky Aaron/Chronicle Books, 1997.

Bill M., O. Mourgue, D. Rams, P. Rosenthal, and M. Zanuso. *Design since 1945*. Exhibition catalogue (Philadelphia, Philadelphia Museum of Art, 16 oct. 1983-8 jan. 1984). Philadelphia: Philadelphia Museum of Art, 1984.

Bonny, A. *Les Années 20*. 2 vol. Paris: Ed. du Regard, 1989.

——. *Les Années 30*. 2 vol. Paris: Ed. du Regard, 1987.

——. *Les Années 50*. Paris: Ed. du Regard, 1982.

——. *Les Années 60*. Paris: Ed. du Regard, 1983.

——. *Les Années 70*. Paris: Ed. du Regard, 1993.

Bosoni, G. *Italy: Contemporary Domestic Landscapes 1945-2000*. Milano: Skira, 2001.

Braden, D. R., R. J. S. Gutman, J. L. Law, W. S. Pretze, H. K. Shramstad, and N. Villa Bryk. *Streamlining America*. Exhibition catalogue (Dearborn, Mi., Henry Ford Museum & Greenfield Village, sett. 1986-dec. 1987). Detroit: Henry Ford Museum & Greenfield Village, 1986.

Braun-Feldweg, W. *Normen und Formen Industrieller Produktion*. Ravensburg: Otto Maier Verlag, 1954.

Brunhammer, Y. *Lo Stile 1925*. Milano: Fratelli Fabbri, 1966

Camber, D., ed. *Mid Century Design Decorative Arts 1940-1960*. Exhibition catalogue (Miami Beach, Bass Museum of Art, 16 nov. 1984-6 jan.1985). Miami Beach: Bass Museum of Art, 1985.

Cariou, J. *Classiques du Design*. Paris: Syros Alternatives, 1988.

Castelli Ferrieri, A., V. Gregotti, P. C. Santini, and P. Tovaglia. *Premio Compasso d'Oro ADI 1970*. Milano: Sisar, 1971.

Central to Design, Central To Industry. Preface by C. Lorentz. London: Central School of Art & Design, 1982.

Centrokappa. *Il Design italiano degli anni '50*. Milano: Ed. Domus, 1989.

Cirio, R. *Qualità, scènes d'objets à l'italienne*. Preface by F. Fellini. Paris: Ed. du May, 1990.

Cornfeld, B., and O Edwards. *Quintessence: The Quality of Having It*. Design by J. C. Jay. New York: Crown Publishers, 1983.

Costantine, M., and A. Drexler. *The Package*. Exhibition catalogue (New York, The Museum of Modern Art, sept.-nov. 1959). New York: The Museum of Modern Art, 1959.

Daniel, G. *Useful Objects Today*. New York: The Museum of Modern Art/Simon & Schuster, s.d.

De Bure, G. *Intérieurs. Le Mobilier français 1965-1979*. Paris: Ed. du Regard, 1983.

De Noblet, J. *Design, Miroir du Siècle*. Exhibition catalogue (Paris, Grand Palais, may-june 1993). Paris: Flammarion-APCI, 1993.

Department of Industrial Design. *The Bulletin of The Museum of Modern Art, New York*, 1 (1946), XIV, pp. 15 and ss.

Le Design Centre de Londres en visite/Het Design Centre Uit Londen Op Bezoek. Bruxelles: 1967.

Le design des années Pop 1960-1973. Folder (Musée des Arts Décoratifs, Paris, june-aug. 1995). Paris: Union Centrale des Arts Décoratifs, 1995.

Design for Use: USA. (XXIe Salon des Arts Ménagers, Grand Palais). Preface by D. Bruce. Paris: Les services des relations culturelles de l'Ambassade des USA, 1952.

Design In America: The Cranbrook Vision 1925-1950. Exhibition catalogue (Detroit, The Detroit Institute of

Art and New York, The Metropolitan Museum of Art). New York: The Detroit Institute of Art/Harry N. Abrams, 1983.

Der Deutsche Industrie-Messe. *Gestaltete Industrieform in Deutschland*. Preface by H. König. Düsseldorf: Econ-Verlag, 1954.

Dooner, K., and S. Steinberg. *Fabulous Fifties: Design for Modern Living*. Atglen, Pa.: Schiffer, 1993.

Dormer, P. *Design since 1945*. London: Thames and Hudson, 1993

Dreyfuss, H. *Industrial Design*. Volume 5. New York: Cooper-Hewitt National Design Museum/Smithsonian Institution/Rizzoli, 1957.

Ducrocq, A. *Formes et Industrie, Label français d'esthétique industrielle*, Institut Français d'Esthétique Industrielle, s.l., 1983.

Edwards, O. *Elegant Solutions: Quintessential Technology for A User-Friendly World*. Photographs by D. Whyte, design by C. J. Jay. New York: Crown Publishers, 1989.

Ellison, M., and L. Pina. *Design for Life: Scandinavian Modern Furnishings 1930-1970*. Atglen, Pa.: Schiffer, 2002.

Ekuan, K. *Design Made In Nippon*. Tokyo: Creo, 1994.

Engler, F., and C. Lichtenstein. *The Esthetics of Minimized Drag Streamlined: a Metaphor for Progress*. Baden: Lars Müller, n.d.

Erlhoff, M., and B. Wolf. *Designed in Germany: Die Anschaulichkeit des Unsichtbaren*. Frankfurt a. M.: Rat für Formgebung/Permanenta, 1988.

———. *Designed in Germany Since 1949*. München: Prestel/Michael Erlhoff, 1990.

Fiell, C. and P. Fiell. *Industrial Design A-Z*. Köln: Benedikt Taschen, 2000.

Fischer, F. and K. B. Hiesinger. *Japanese Design: A Survey Since 1950*. Exhibition catalogue (Philadelphia, Philadelphia Museum of Art, 25 sept.-20 nov. 1994). New York: Harry N. Abrams, 1994.

Forme Nuove in Italia, New Forms in Italy. Preface by A. Pica. Milano: Bestetti, 1962.

Forty, A. *Objects of Desire: Design and Society since 1750*. London: Thames and Hudson, 1986.

Frateili, E. *Design e civiltà della macchina*. Roma: Editalia, 1969.

Gardiner, J. *From the Bomb to the Beatles: The Changing Face of Post War Britain 1945-1965*. London: Collins & Brown, 1999.

Greenberg, C. *Mid-Century Modern: Furniture of the 1950s*. London:

Thames and Hudson, 1984.

———. *Op to Pop Furniture of the 1960's*; Boston: Bulfinch Press, 1984.

Greif, M. *Depression Modern: The Thirties Style in America*. New York: Universe, 1975.

Guilfoyle, B. *Portable World*. Exhibition catalogue (New York, The Museum of Contemporary Crafts of the American Crafts Council, 5 oct. 1973-1 jan. 1974). Houston: The Museum of Contemporary Crafts of the American Crafts Council, 1973.

Hatje, G., and U. Hatje, U. *Design for Modern Living*. New York: Harry N. Abrams, 1962.

Heide, R., and Gilman, J. *Dime-Store Dream Parade: Popular Culture 1925-1955*. Photographs by L. Otway. New York: E. P. Dutton, 1979.

Heinz, H., *Gestalten für die Serie, Design in der DDR 1949-1985*. Dresden: VEB, 1988.

Hennesey, W. J. *Modern Furnishings for The Home*. New York: Reinhold Publishing, 1952.

Herbst, R. *25 années Uam 1930-1955, Les formes utiles: l'architecture, les arts plastiques, les arts graphiques, le mobilier, l'équipement ménager*. Paris: Ed. du Salon des Arts Ménagers, 1956.

Hess, A. *Googie: Fifties Coffe Shop Architecture*, Chronicle Books, San Francisco, 1986.

Hiesinger, K. B., and G. H. Marcus. *Landmarks of Twentieth-Century Design: an Illustrated Handbook*, New York: Abbeville Press, 1993.

Higgins, K., *Collecting The 1970s*, Miller's, London, 2001.

Hillier, B. *The Style of The Century*. 2nd ed. London: Watson Guptill, 1998.

Hine, T. *Populuxe: the Look and Life of America in the 50's and 60's from Tailfins and Tv Dinners to Barbie Dolls and Fallout Shelters*. New York: Alfred A. Knopf, 1990.

History of Industrial Design 1919-1990: The Dominion of Design. Milano: Electa, 1991.

Horn, R. *Fifties Style*. New York: Friedman/Fairfax, 1993.

Hulten, K. G. P. *The Machine as Seen at the End of the Mechanical Age*. Exhibition catalogue (New York, The Museum of Modern Art 25 nov. 1968-9 feb. 1969). New York: The Museum of Modern Art, 1968.

I'll Buy That! 50 Small Wonders and Big Deals that Revolutionized the Lives of Consumers. Preface by R. H. Karpatkin. Mount Vernon, NY: Consumers Union, 1986.

Jackson, L. *The New Look Design*

in the Fifties. London: Thames and Hudson, 1991.

———. *The Sixties: Decade of Design Revolution*. London: Phaidon Press, 1998.

Jeffrey, I., and A. J. P Taylor. *Thirties: British Art and Design Before the War*. Exhibition catalogue (Hayward Gallery, London, 25 oct. 1979-13 jan. 1980). London: Arts Council of Great Britain, 1979.

Johns, B. *Jet Dreams: Art of The Fifties in the Northwest*. Exhibition catalogue (Tacoma, Tacoma Art Museum, march-june 1995). Seattle: Tacoma Art Museum/University of Washington Press, 1995.

Johnson, P. *Design 1935-1965: What Modern Was (Selections from The Liliane and David M. Stewart Collection)*. Edited by M. Heidelberg. New York: Harry N. Abrams/Le Musée des Arts Décoratifs de Montréal, 1991.

The Junior Council of The Museum of Modern Art. *The Design Collection: Selected Objects*. New York: The Museum of Modern Art, 1970.

Kaufmann Jr., E. *Industrie und Handwerk Schaffen/Neues Hausgerät in USA*. Berlin: Saul Steinberg, 1951.

Kepes, G. *Language Of Vision*. Chicago: Paul Theobald, 1959.

Klatt, J. and G. Staeffler. *Braun + Design Collection: 40 Jahre Braun Design 1955 bis 1995*. n.p.: 1995.

Klöcker, J. *Zeitgemäße Form. Industrial Design International*. München: Süddeutscher Verlag, 1967.

Linz, J. *Art Deco Chrome*. Atglen, Pa.: Schiffer, 1999.

Lippincott J. G. *Design for Business*, Chicago: Paul Theobald, 1947.

Machine Art. Facsimile of the exhibition catalogue (New York, The Museum of Modern Art, mar.-apr. 1934). Anniversary edition. Preface by P. Johnson. New York: The Museum of Modern Art, 1994.

Marcus, G. H. *Design in the Fifties: When Everyone Went Modern*. München: Prestel, 1998.

Marling, K. A. *As Seen on TV: The Visual Culture of Everyday Life in the 1950s*. Cambridge, Mass. - London: Harvard University Press, 1994.

Marsh, M. *Collecting The 1950s*. London: Miller's, 1997.

———. *Collecting The 1960s*. London: Miller's, 1999.

Matami, Y. *Sony Design 1950-1992*. Tokyo: Asahi Sonorama, 1993.

Meikle, J. L. *Twentieth Century Limited Industrial Design in America: 1925-1939*. Philadelphia: Temple University, 1979.

Nichols, S., assisted by E. Agro and E. Teller. *Aluminum by Design*. Exhibition catalogue (Carnegie Museum of Art, Pittsburgh, Pa.). Essays by P. Antonelli, D. P. Doordan, R. Friedel, P. Sparke, C. Vogel. New York: Carnegie Museum of Art/Harry N. Abrams, 2001.

Novy, P. *Housework without Tears*, London: Pilot Press, 1945.

Ockner, P., and L. Pina. *Art Deco Aluminum: Kensington*. Atglen, Pa.: Schiffer, 1997

Paramonik, D. *L'Expo 58 et Le Style Atome*. Preface by A. Massaki. Bruxelles: Magic-Strip, 1983.

Patrix, G. *Beauté ou Laideur ? Vers une esthétique industrielle*. Paris: Hachette, 1967

Pearce, C. *The Fifties: A Pictorial Review*. London: Blossom, 1991

———. *Fifties: le Style des Années 50*. n.p.: 1994.

———. *Twentieth Century Design Classics: From the Anglepoise Lamp to the Zippo Lighter*. London: Blossom, 1991.

Peel, L., and P. Powell. *50s and 60s Style*. n.p.: Chartwell Books Inc., Edison, NJ, 1988.

Pilgrim, D. H., D. Tashjian, and R. G. Wilson. *Machine Age in America 1918-1941*. Exhibition catalogue (Los Angeles, Los Angeles County Museum of Art, 16 aug.-18 oct. 1987). New York: Harry N. Abrams, 1986.

Pina, L. *Fifties Furniture*. Atglen, Pa.: Schiffer, 1996.

Pulos, A. J. *The American Design Adventure: 1940-1975*. Cambridge, Mass. - London: MIT Press, 1988.

Read, H. *Art and Industry: the Principle of Industrial Design*. London: Faber & Faber, 1954.

Ritchie, A. C. *Good Design Is Your Business*. Buffalo: Holling Press, 1947.

Seit Langem Bewährt. München: Museum für Angewandte Kunst, 1968.

Sexton, R. *American Style Classic Product Design from Airstream to Zippo*. San Francisco: Chronicle Books, 1987.

The Society of Industrial Artists and Designers. *Designers in Britain 5*. London: Universe, 1957.

The Society of Industrial Artists and Designers, *Designers in Britain 6: A Review of Graphic and Industrial Design*. London: The Society of Industrial Artists and Designers/David Kaplan, 1964.

Society of Industrial Designers. *US Industrial Design: 1949-1950*. New York: The Studio Publications, 1949.

Society of Industrial Designers. *US Industrial Design 1951*. New York: The Studio Publications & Thomas Y. Crowell, 1951.

Society of Industrial Designers. *Industrial Design in America 1954*. New York: Farrar, Straus and Young, 1954.

Sparke, P. *Design Directory Great Britain*. Bristol: Pavilion, 2001

———. *Electrical Appliances: Twentieth Century Design*. Bristol: 1987.

Stéphane, L. *Chronologie du Design*, Flammarion, Paris 1999.

Taschen, B. *50s Design: 30 Postcards*. Köln: Benedikt Taschen, 1993.

Trentacinque Mobili del Razionalismo Italiano. Mobili come Aforismi. Catalogue of the "Salone del Mobile di Milano" (Milano, 1988). Milano: Electa, 1988.

US Departement of Commerce. *Design USA: Packaging and Corporate Graphics*. n.p.: 1965.

"Useful Objects in Wartime", in *The Bulletin of The Museum of Modern Art, New York*, 2 (December 1942-January 1943), X, pp. 23 and ss.

Van Doren, H. *Industrial Design*. 10th ed. New York: McGraw-Hill, 1940.

Wright, R. *Good Design Is for Everyone - in His Own Words*. New York: Manitoga/The Russel Wright Design Center/Universe, 2001.

———. *Guide to Easier Living*. 2nd reprint. New York: Simon & Schuster, 1951.

Yelavich, S. *Design for Life*. New York: Cooper-Hewitt National Design Museum/Smithsonian Institution/Rizzoli, 1997.

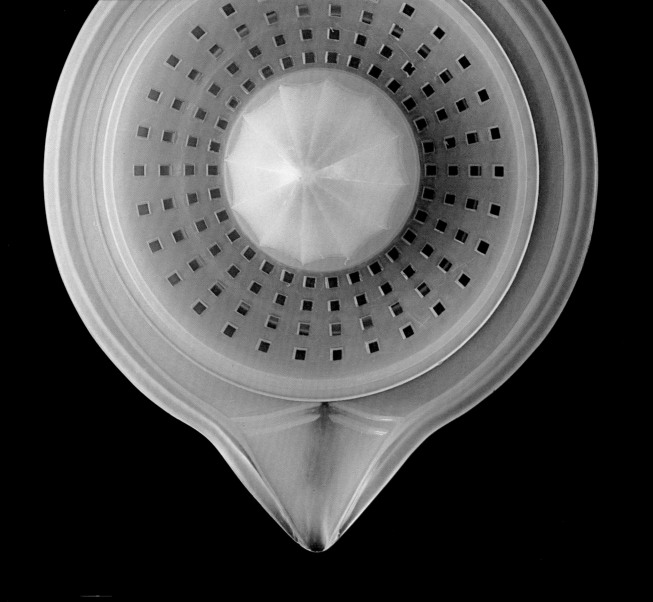

Drinking

Eating

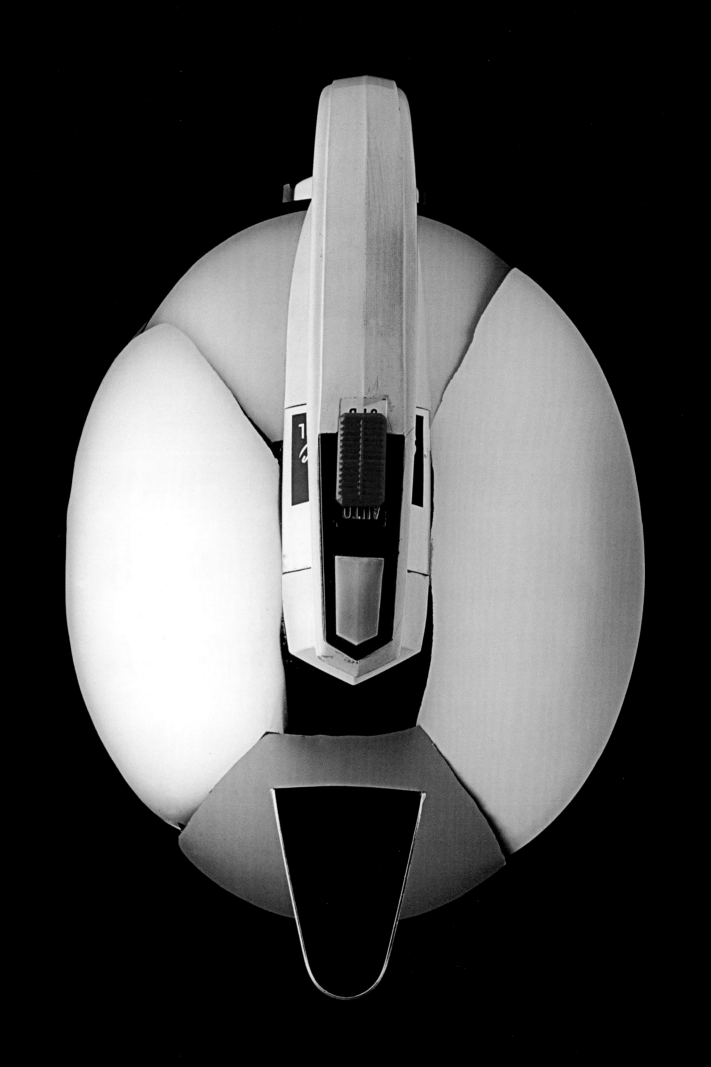

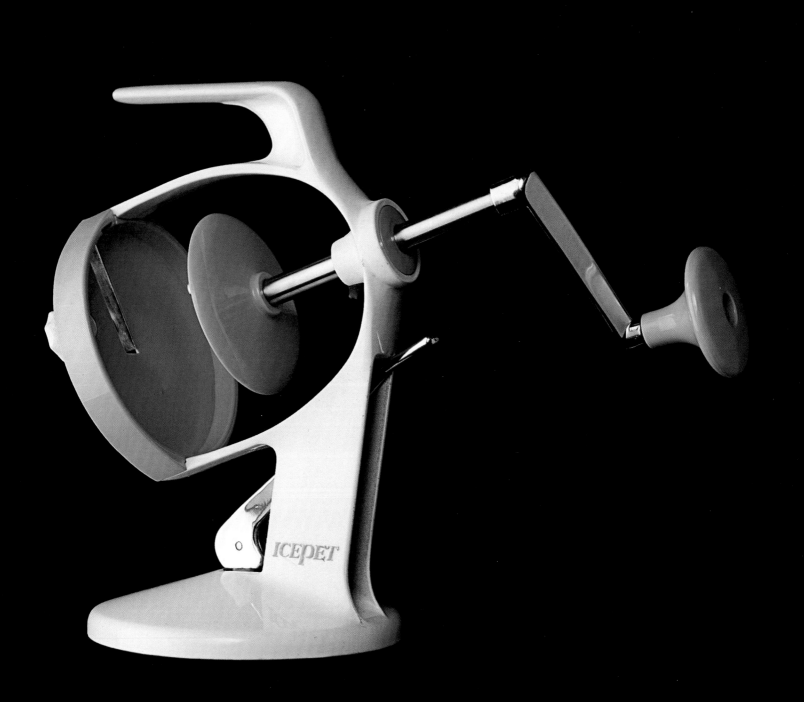

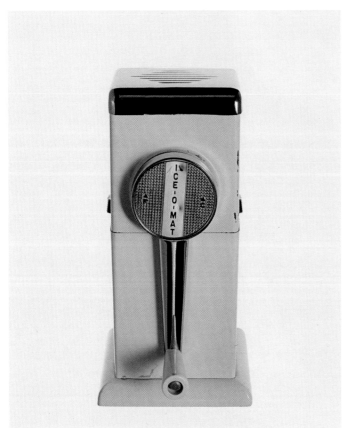

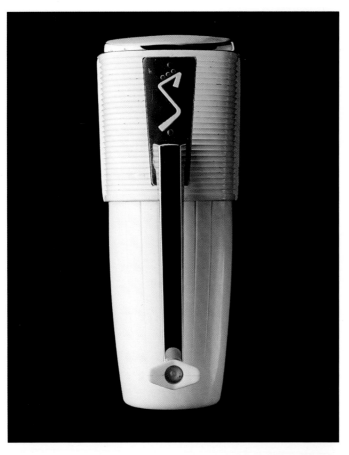

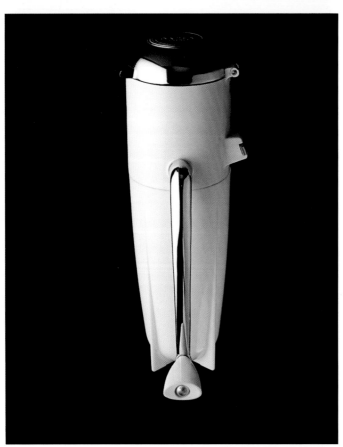
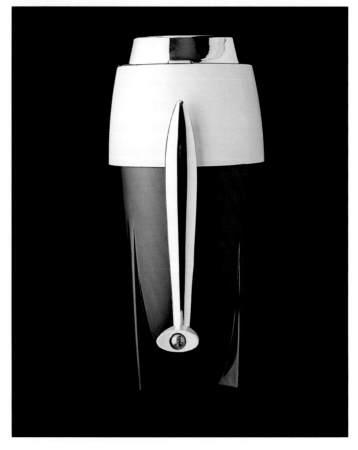

44

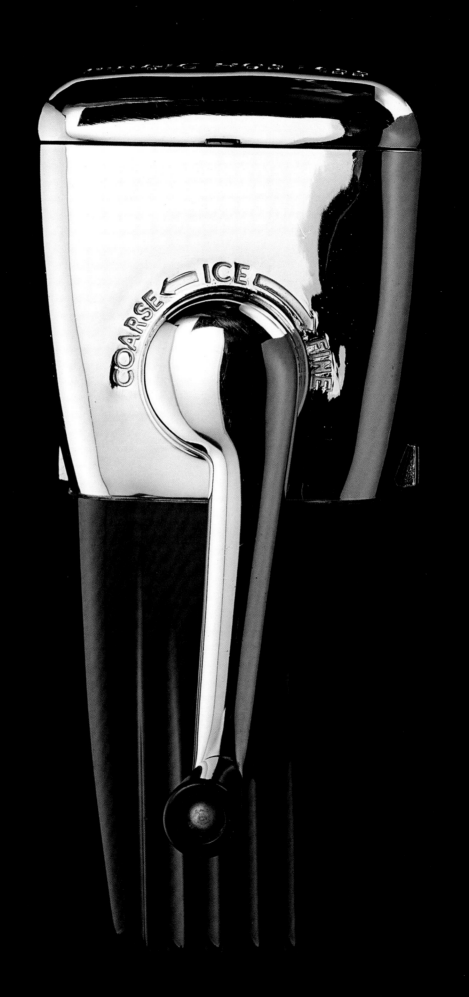

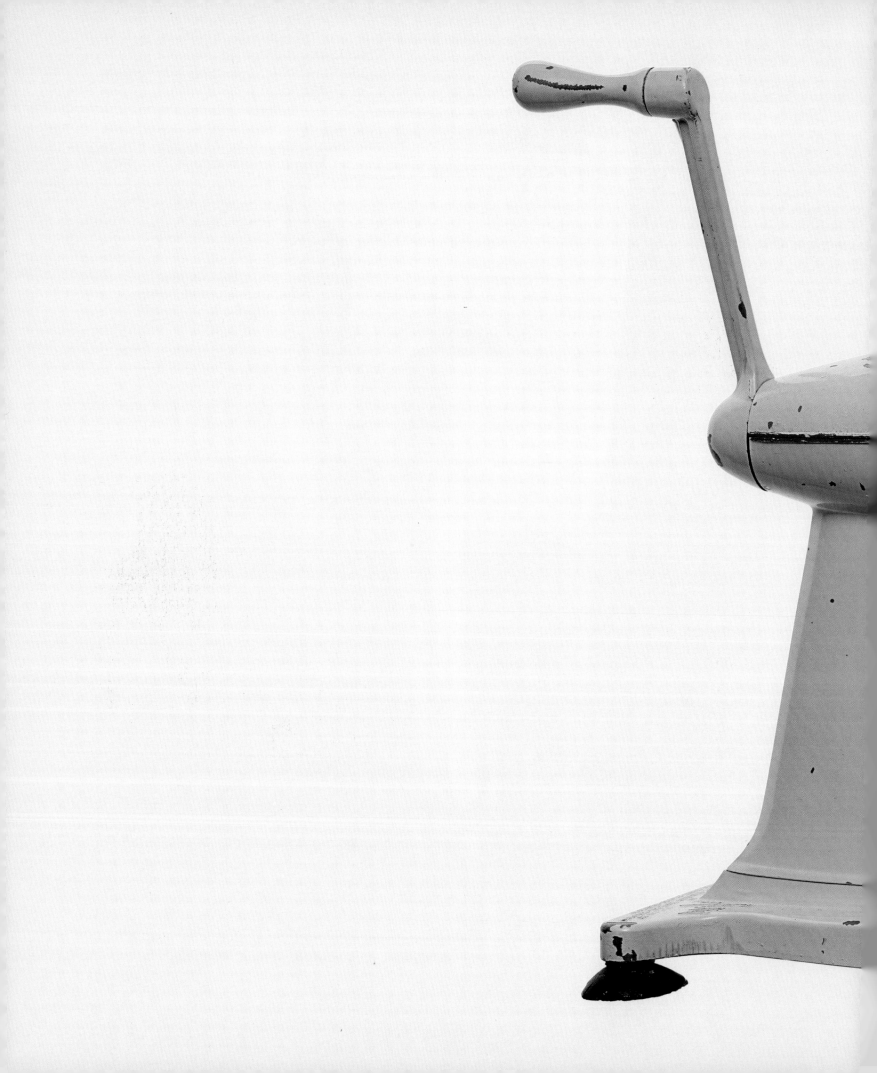

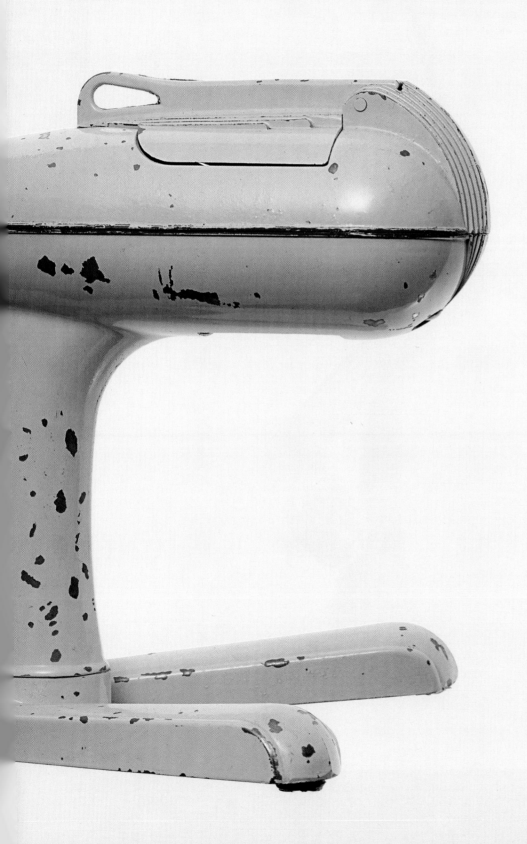

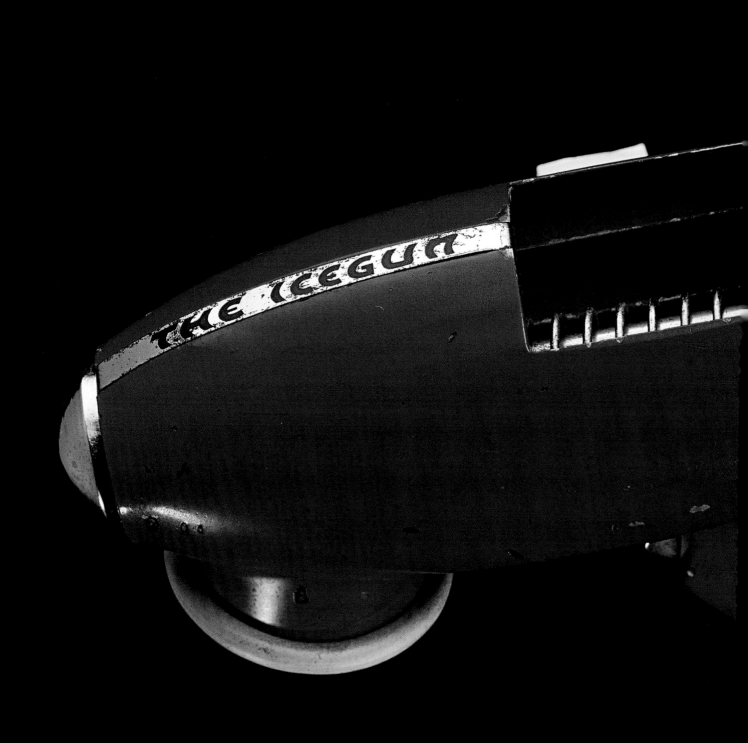

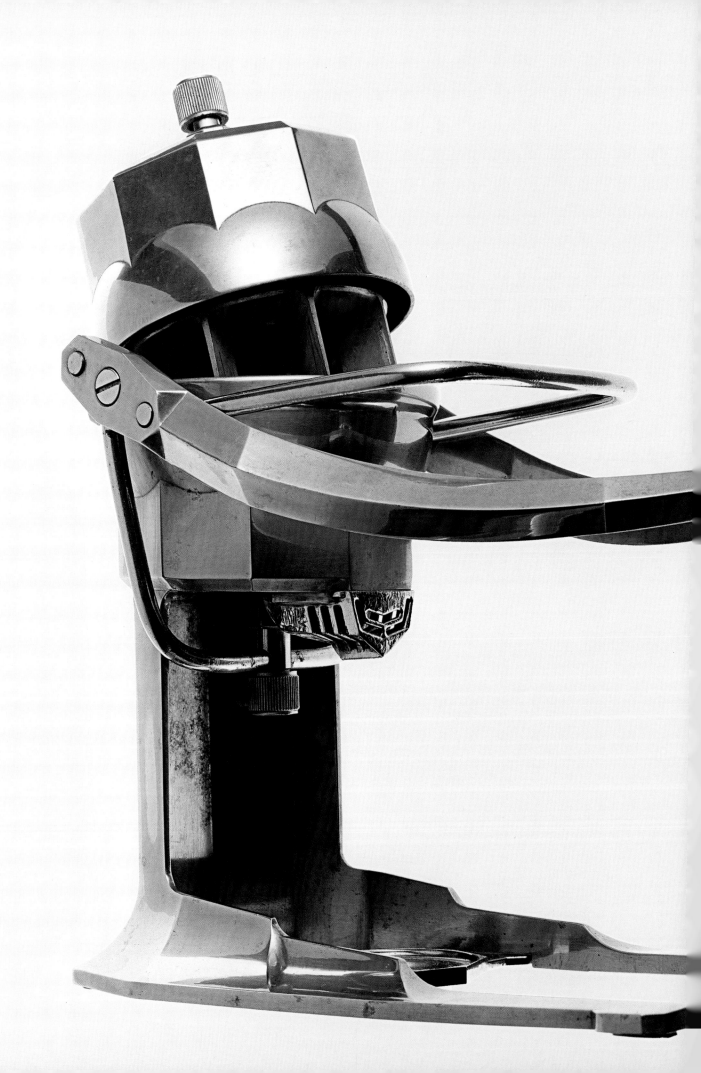

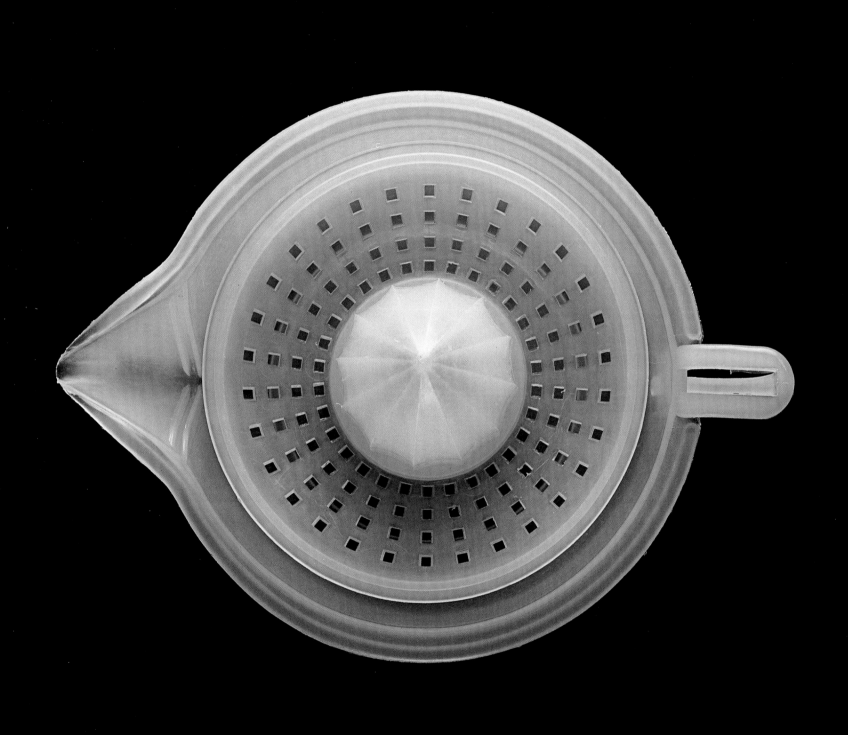

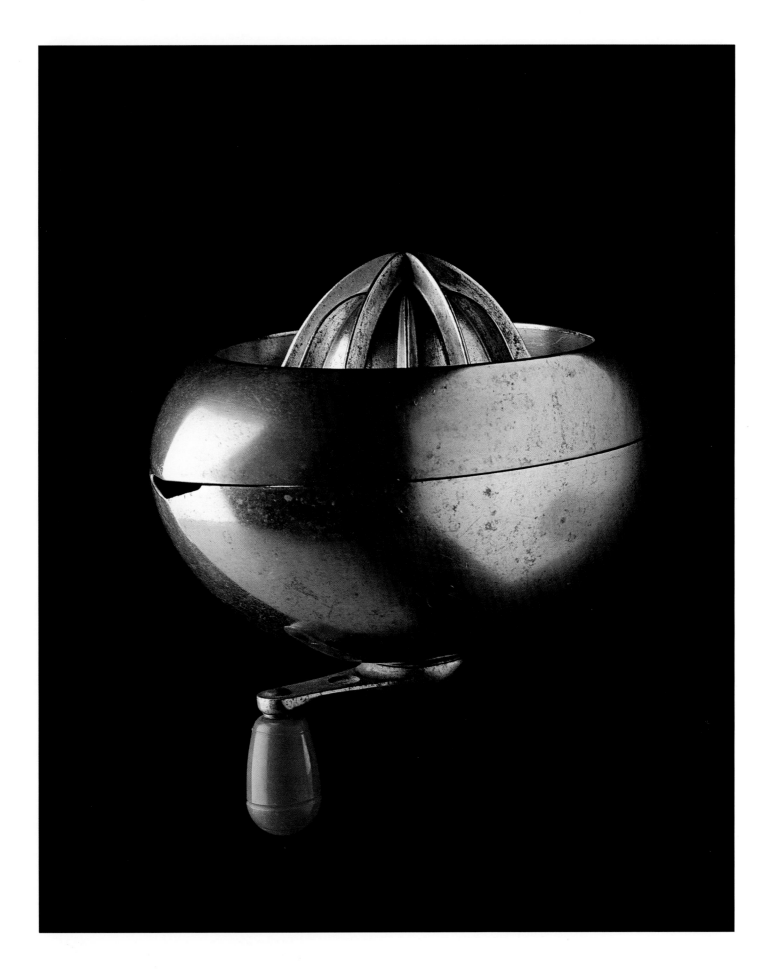

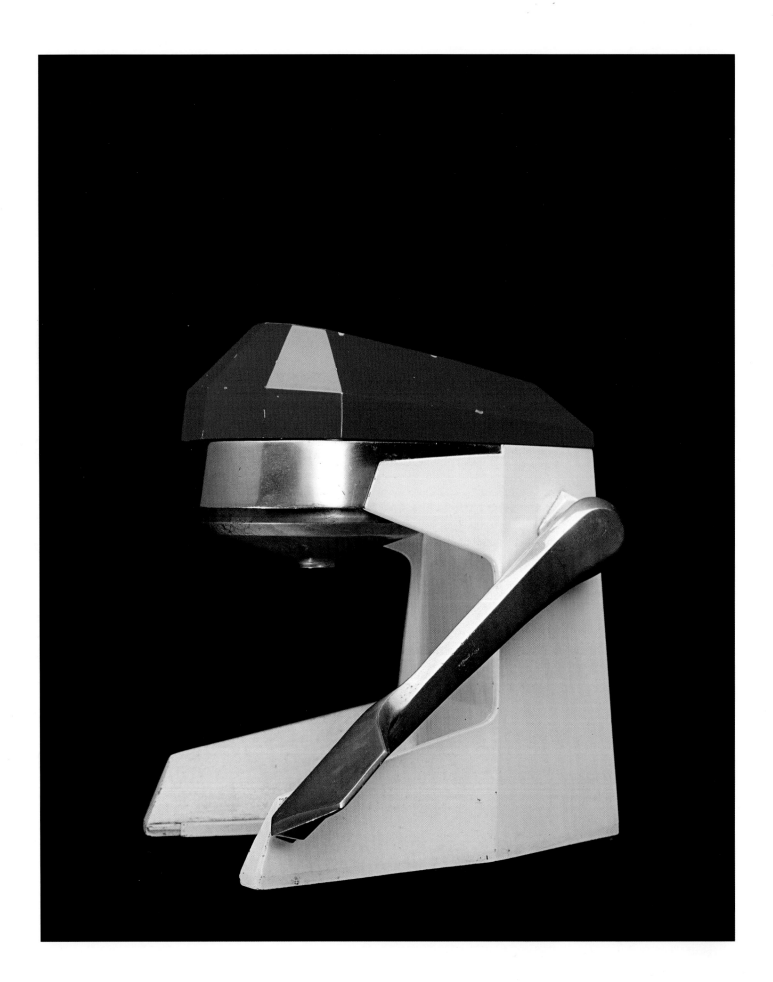

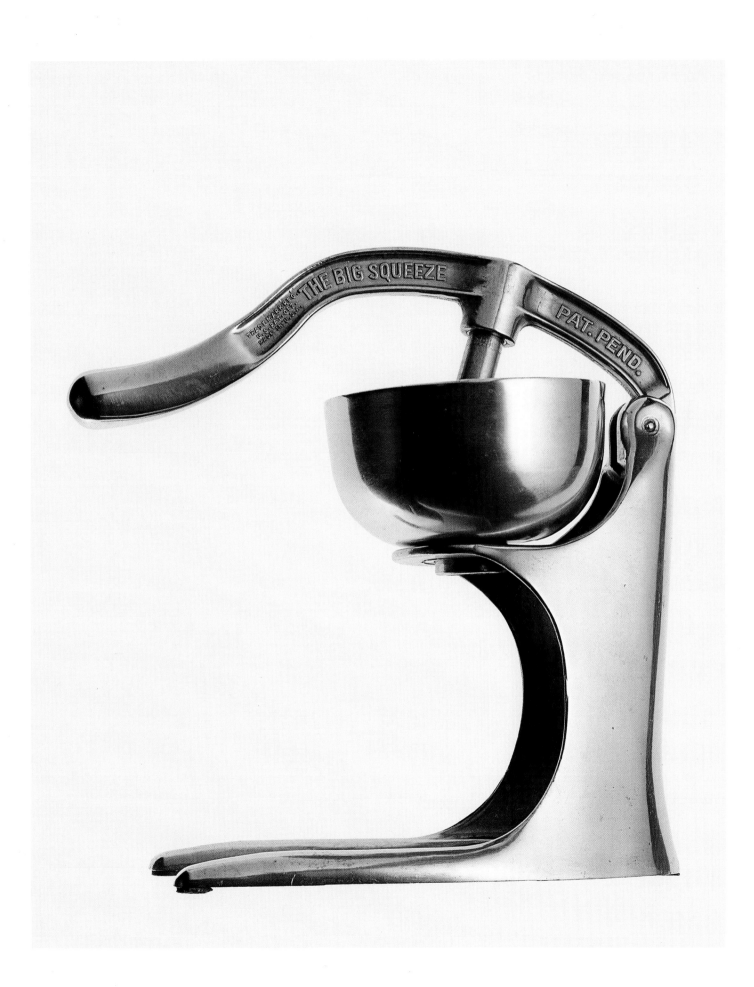

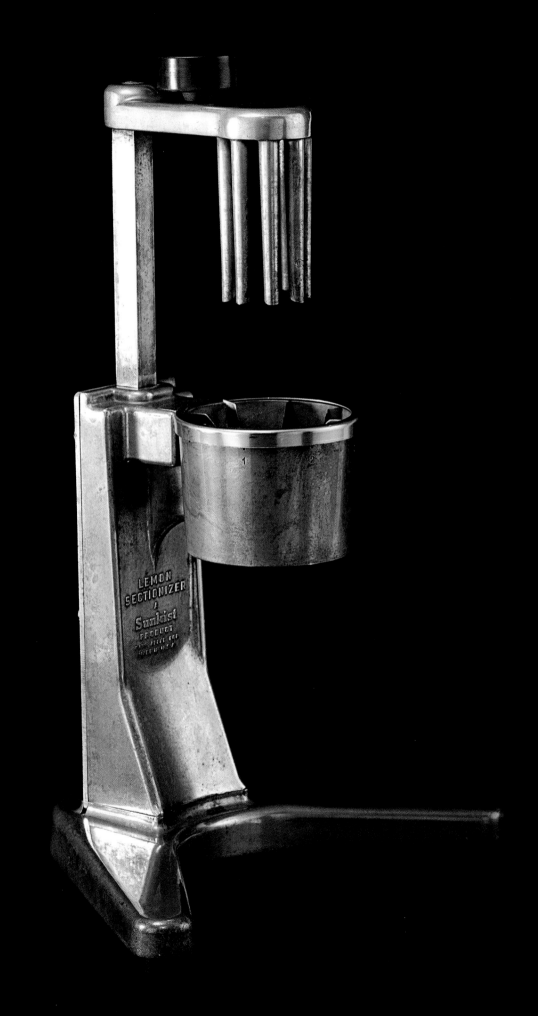

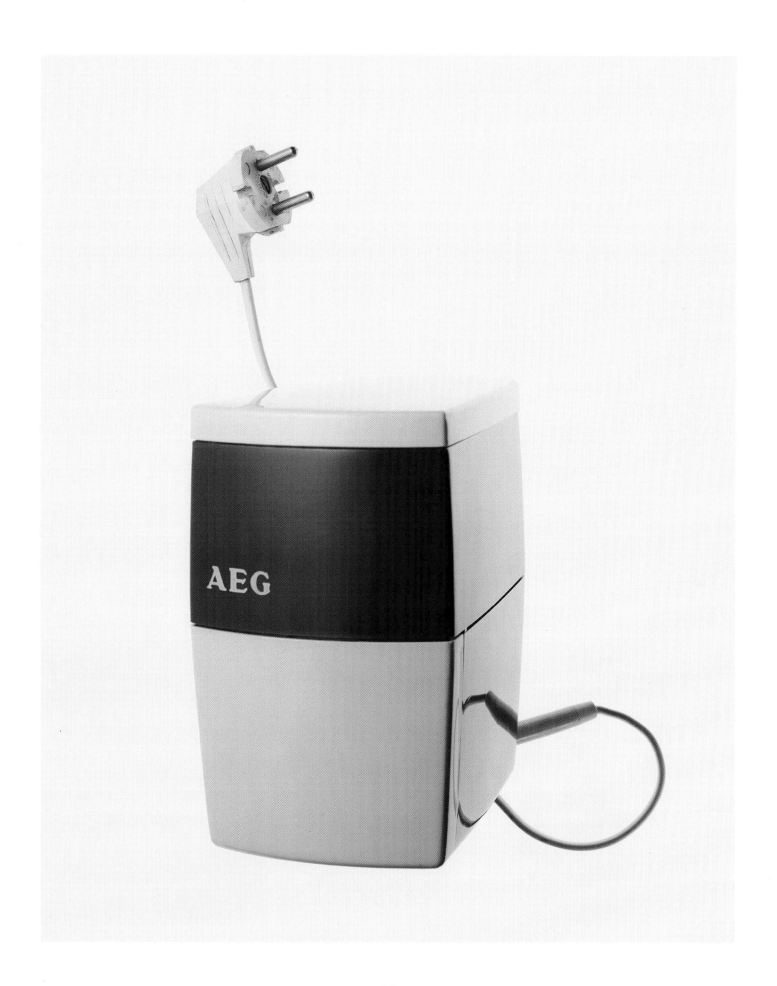

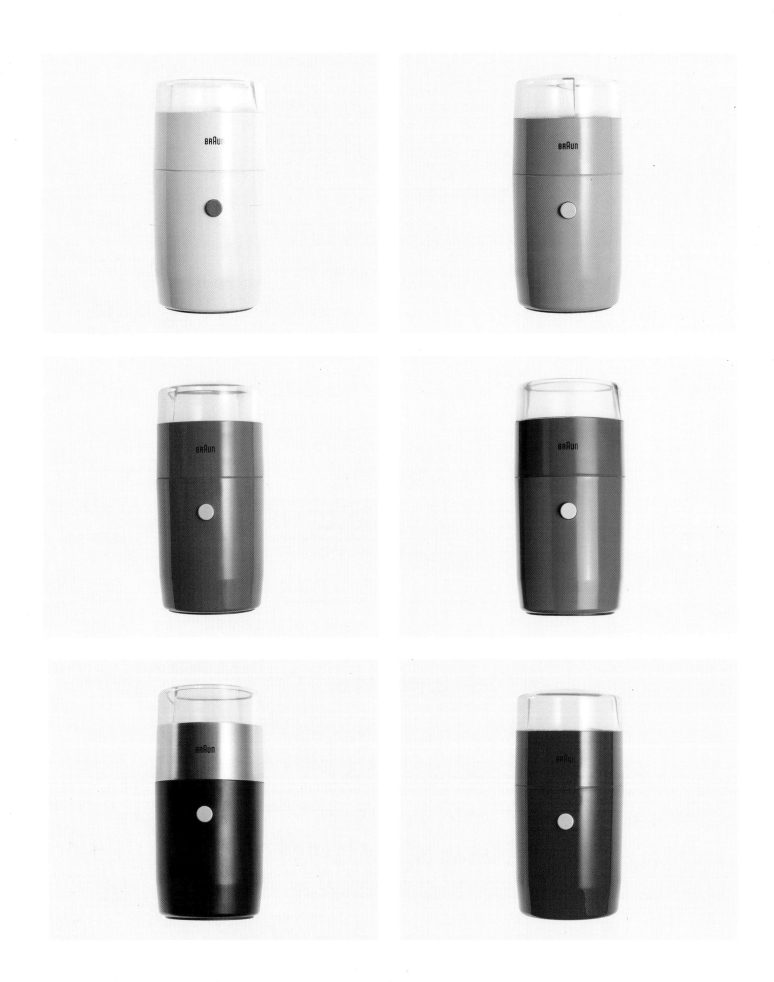

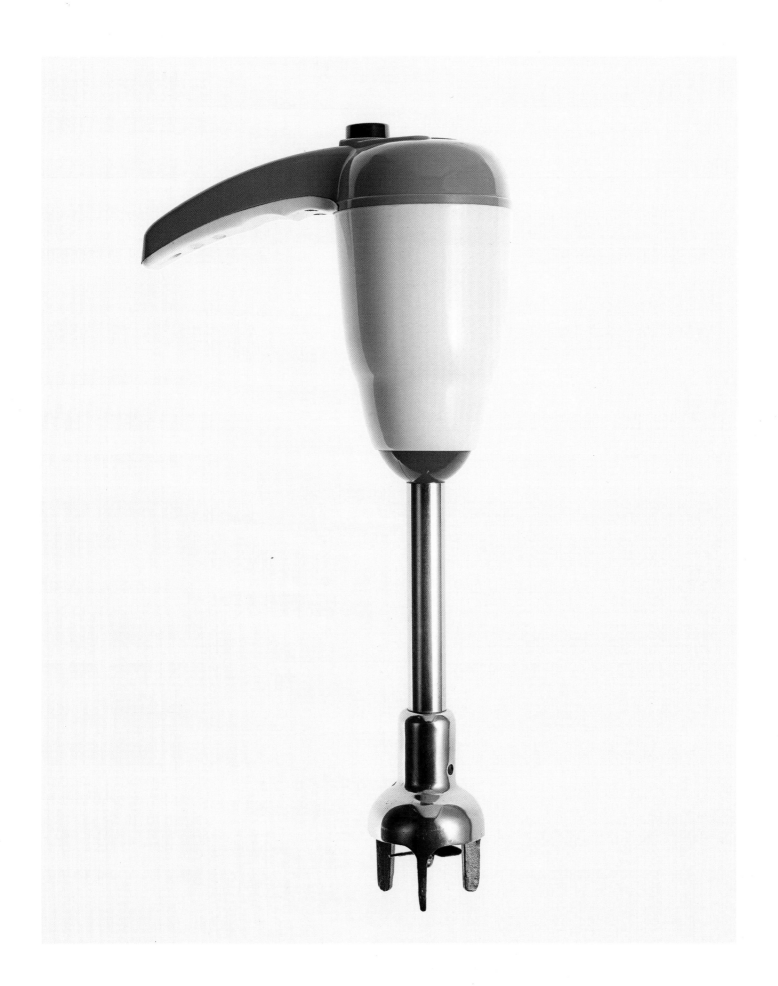

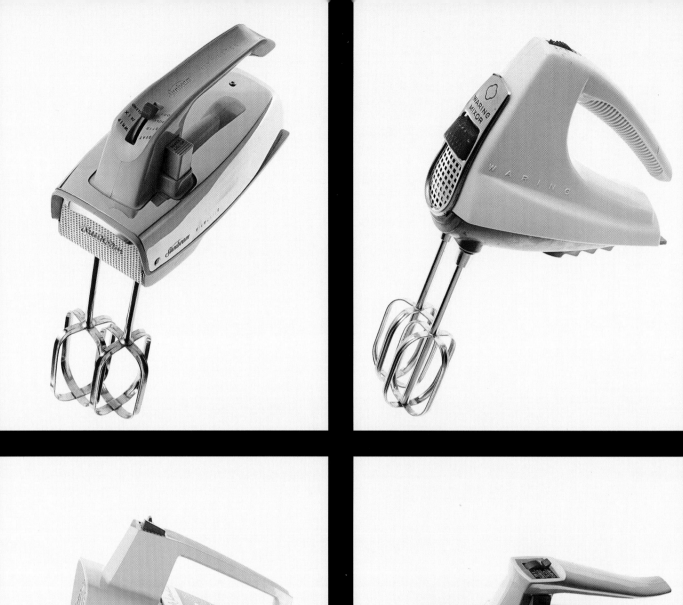
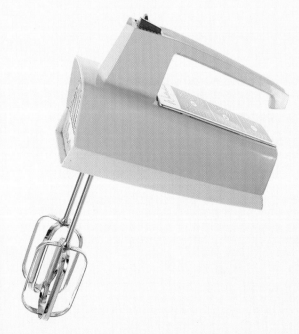

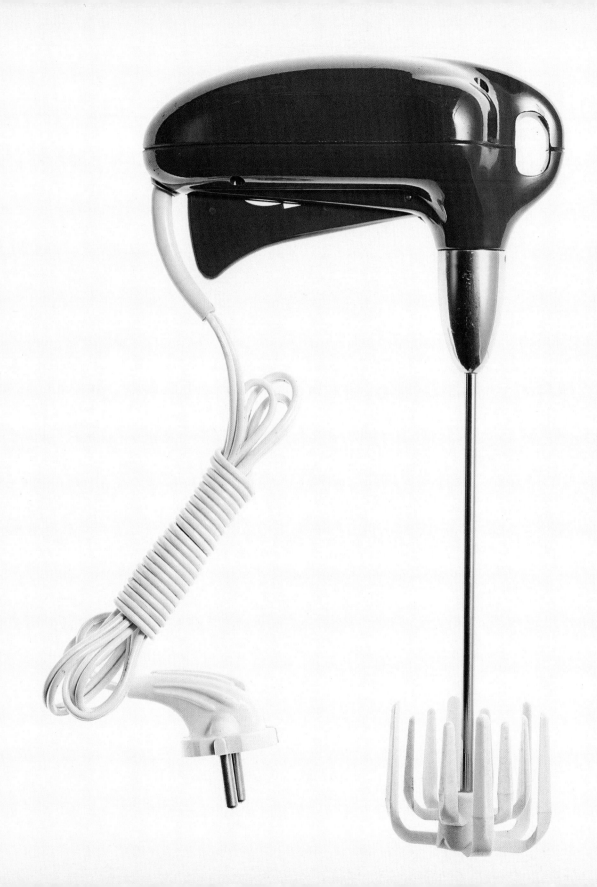

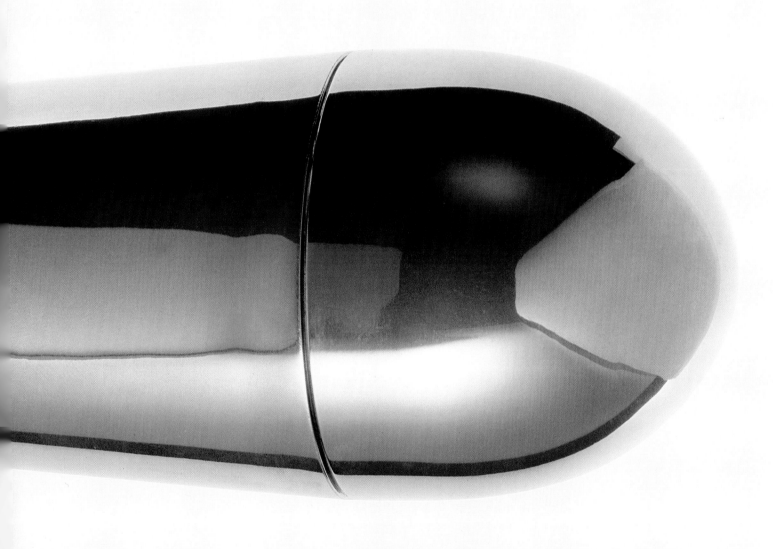

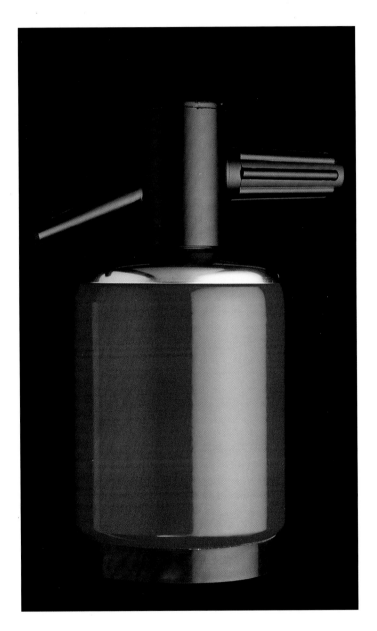

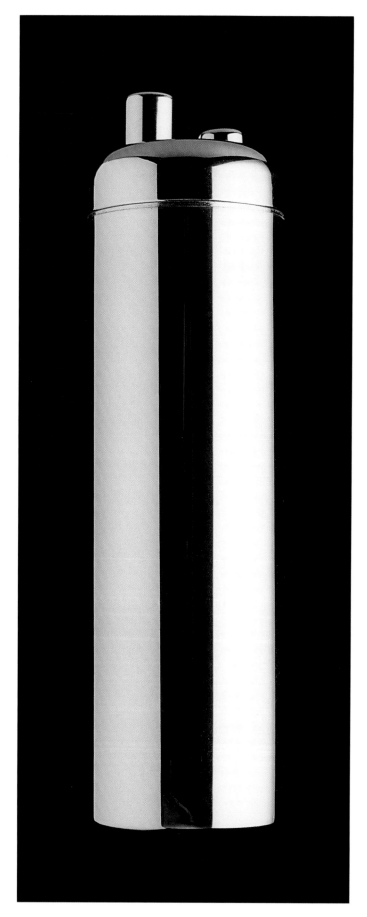

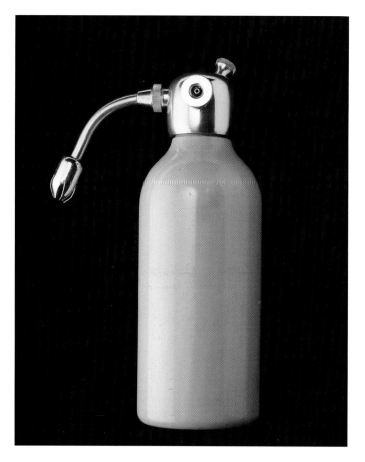

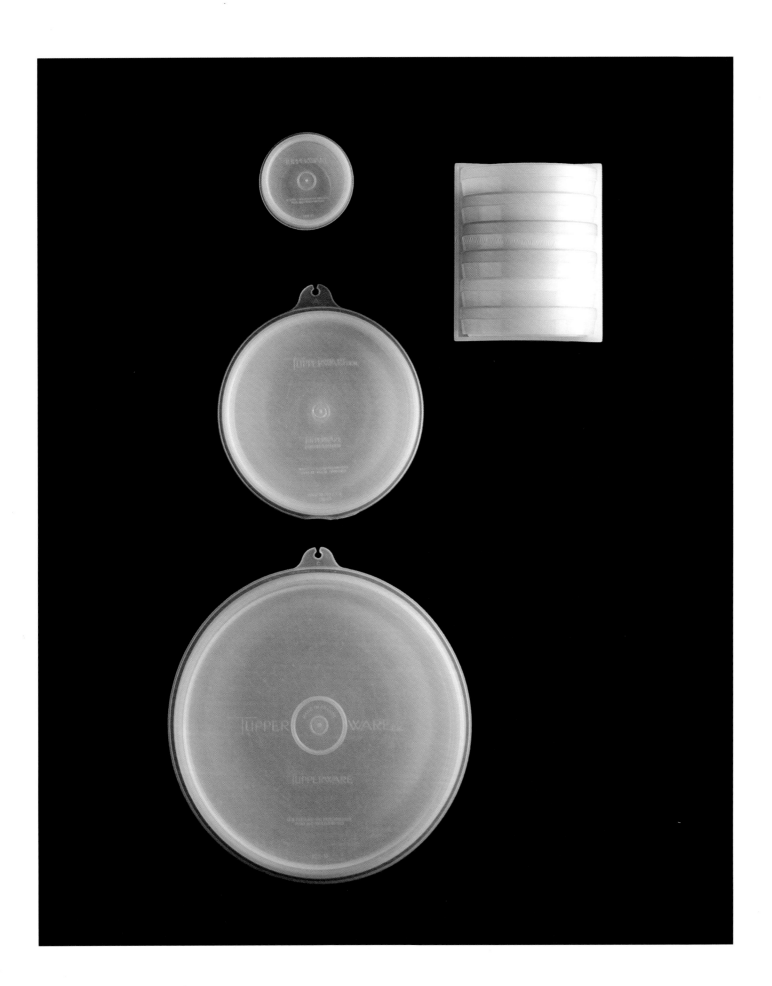

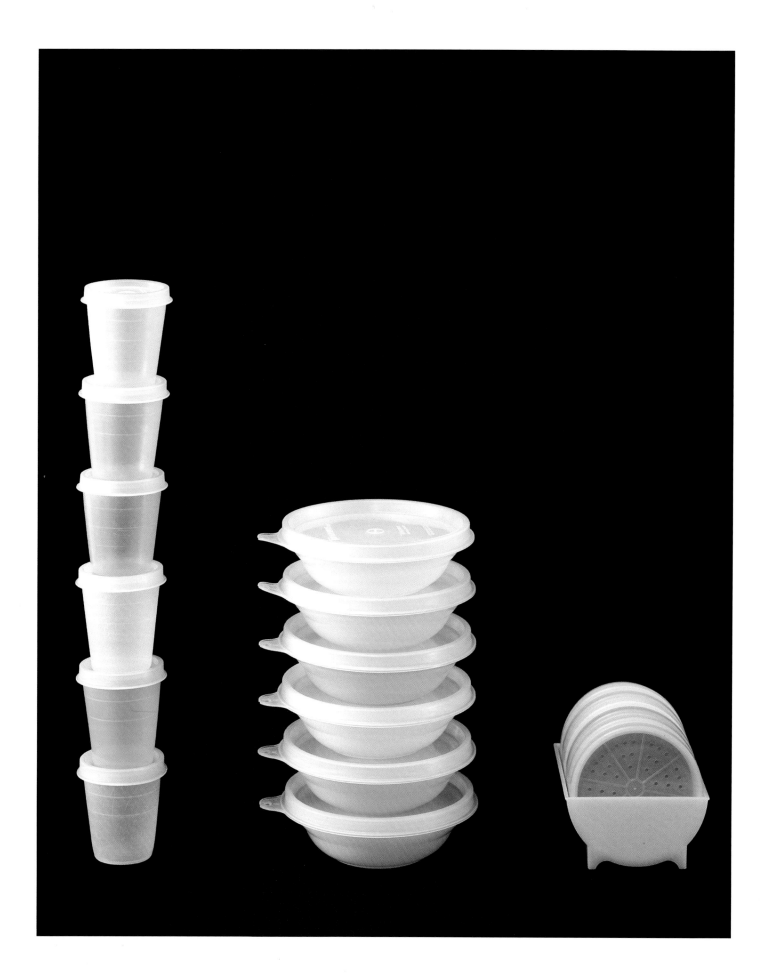

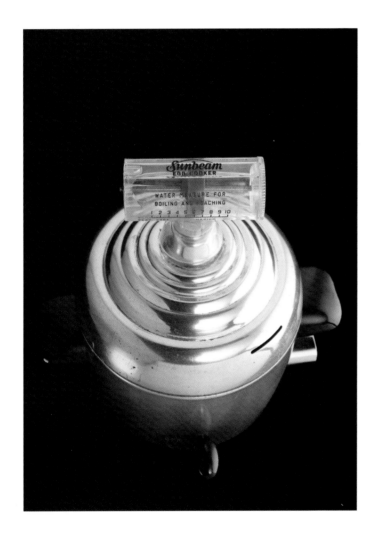

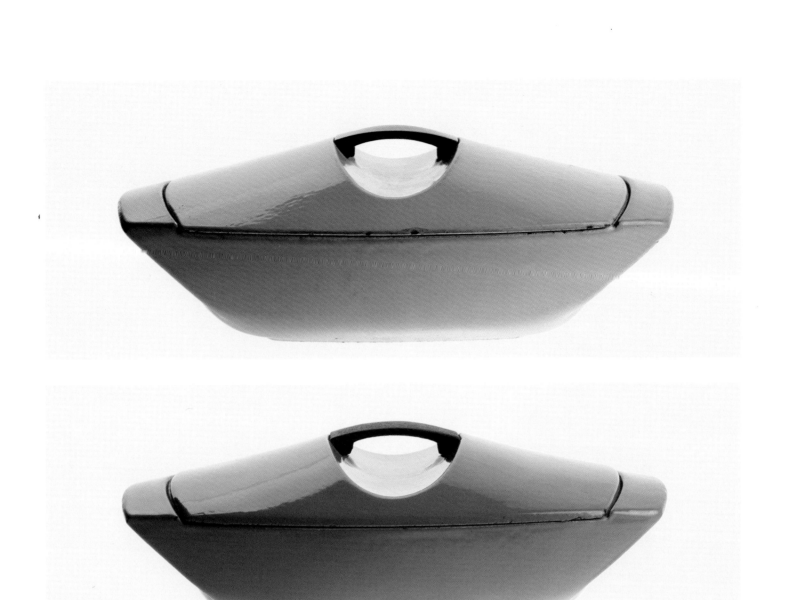

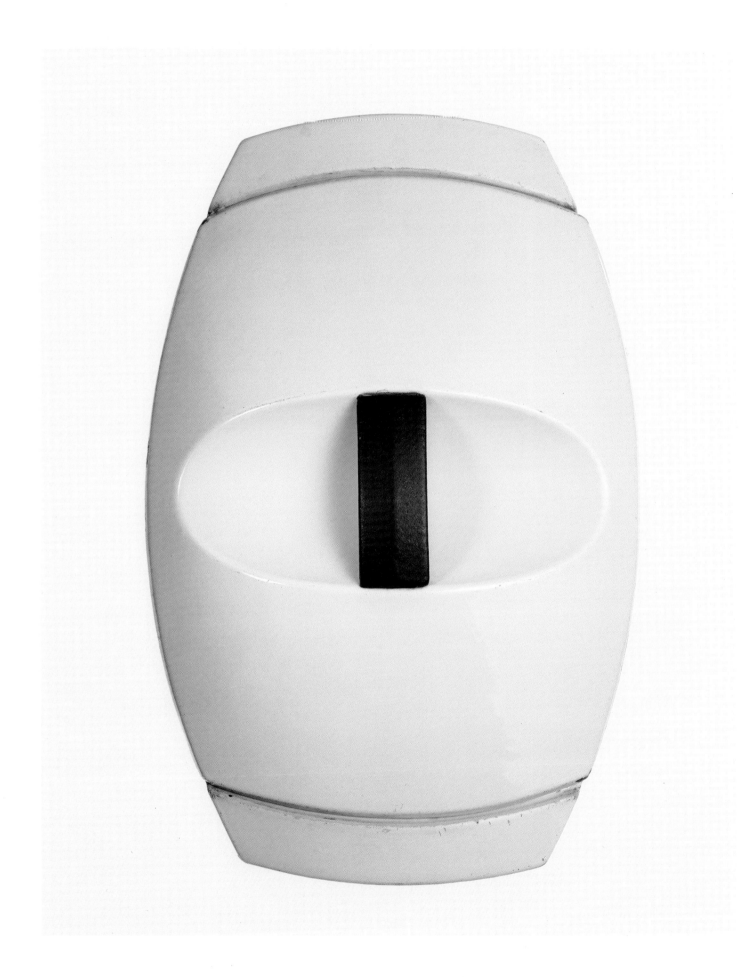

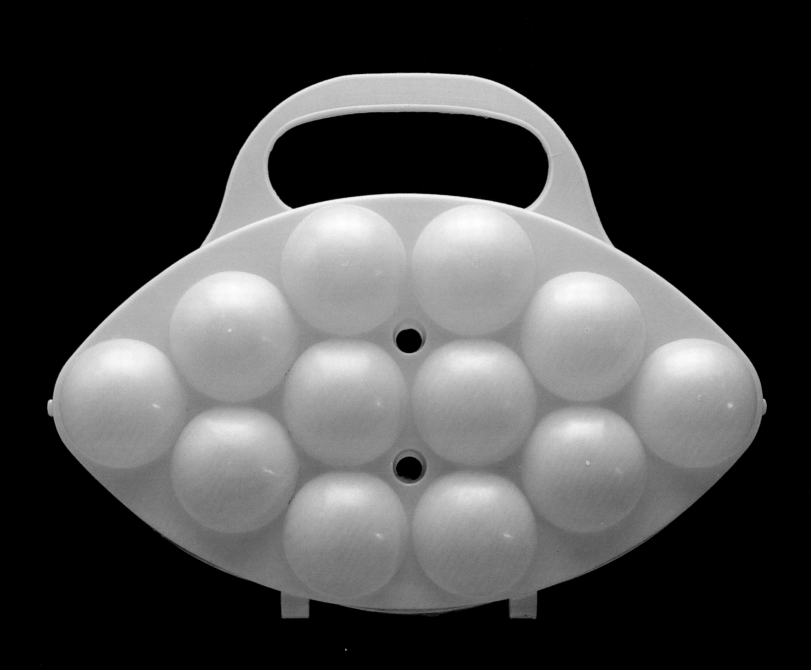

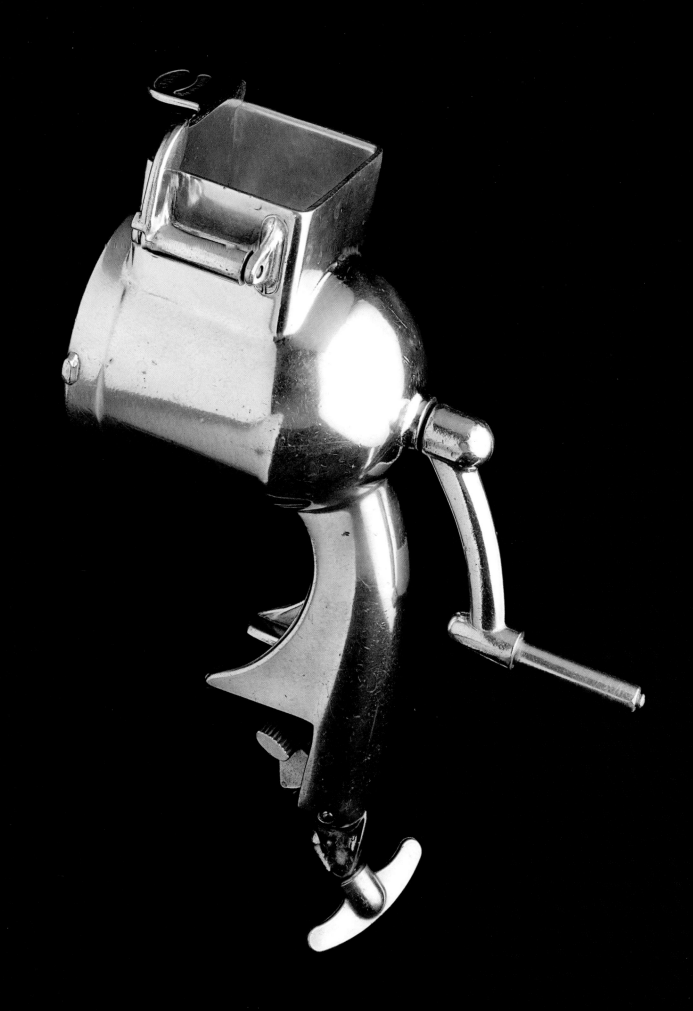

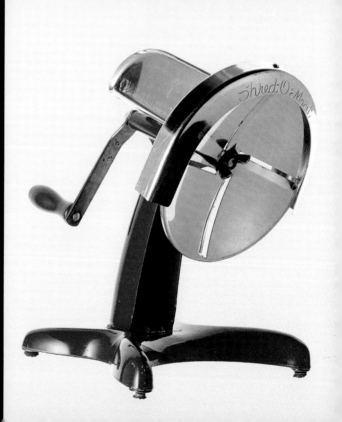

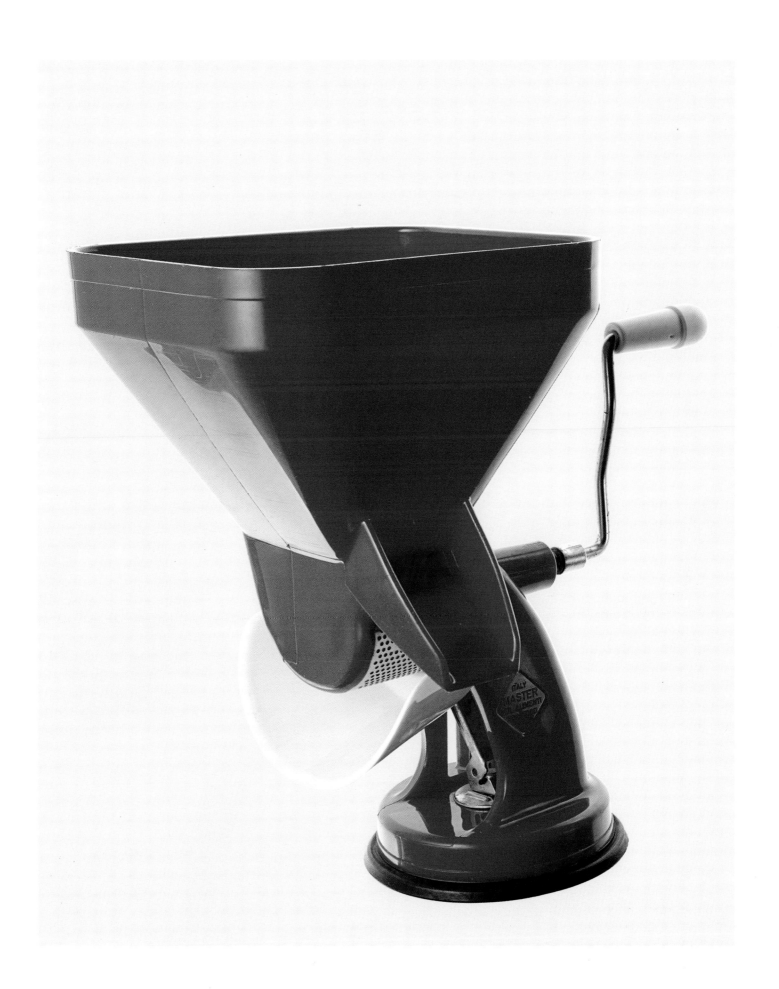

215

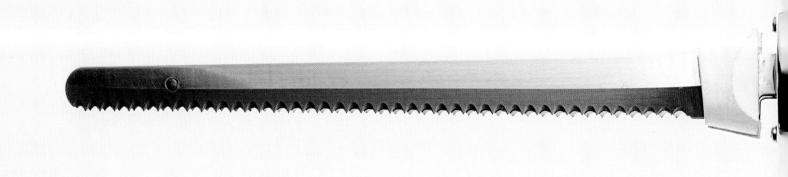
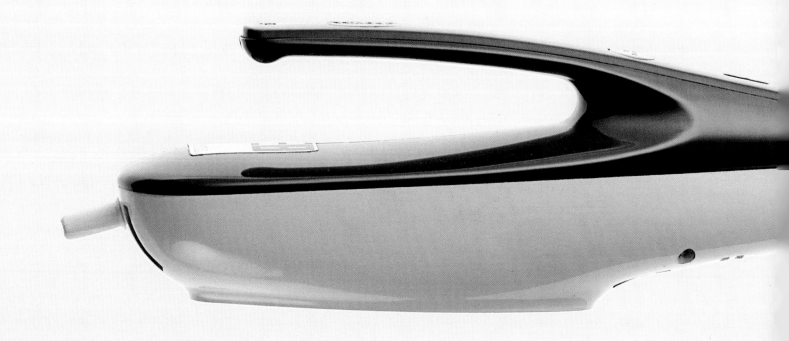

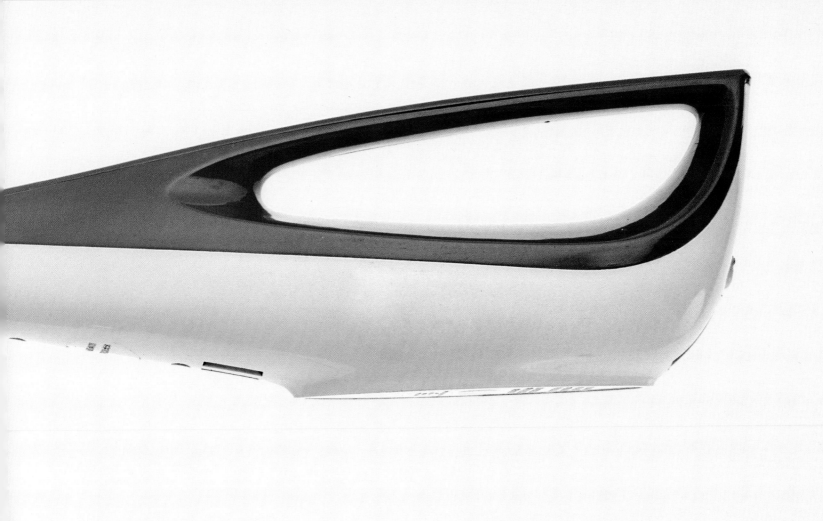

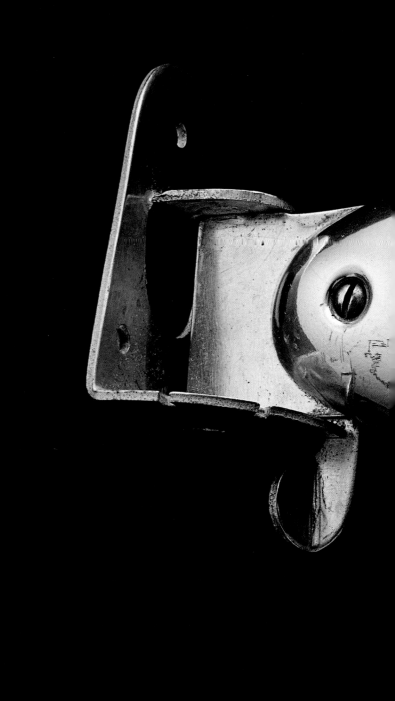

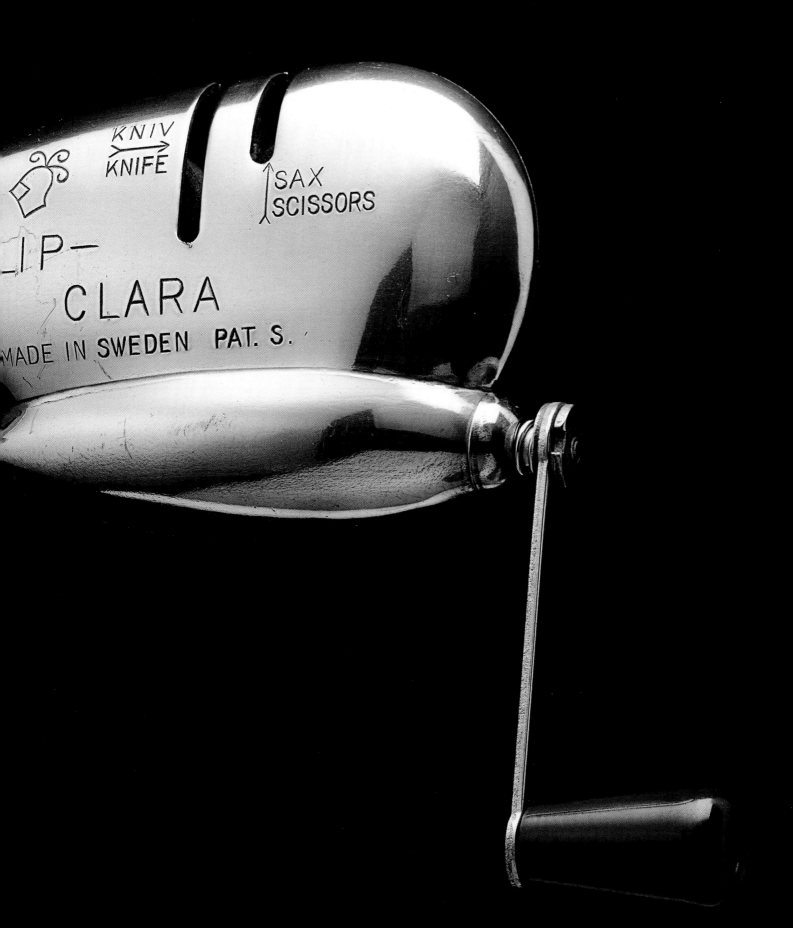

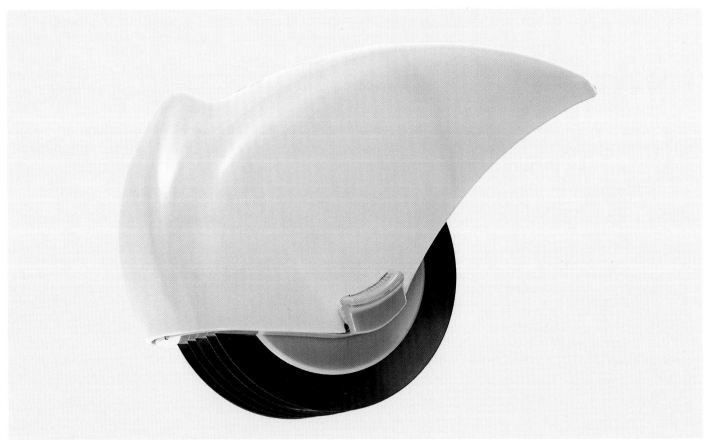

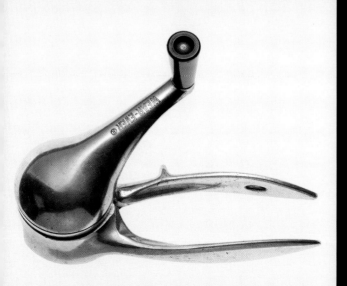

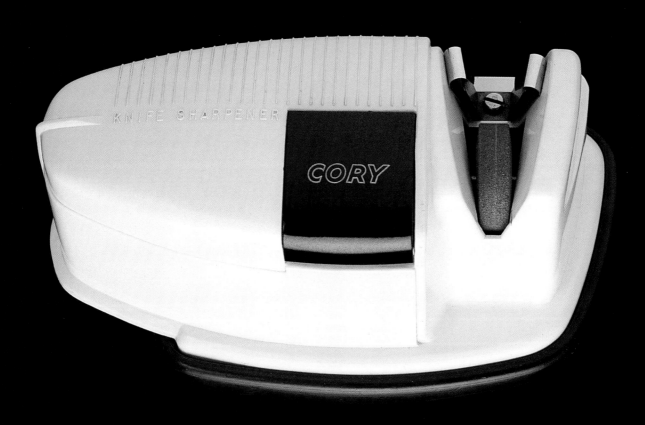

Heating

Cooling

Heaters
Fans

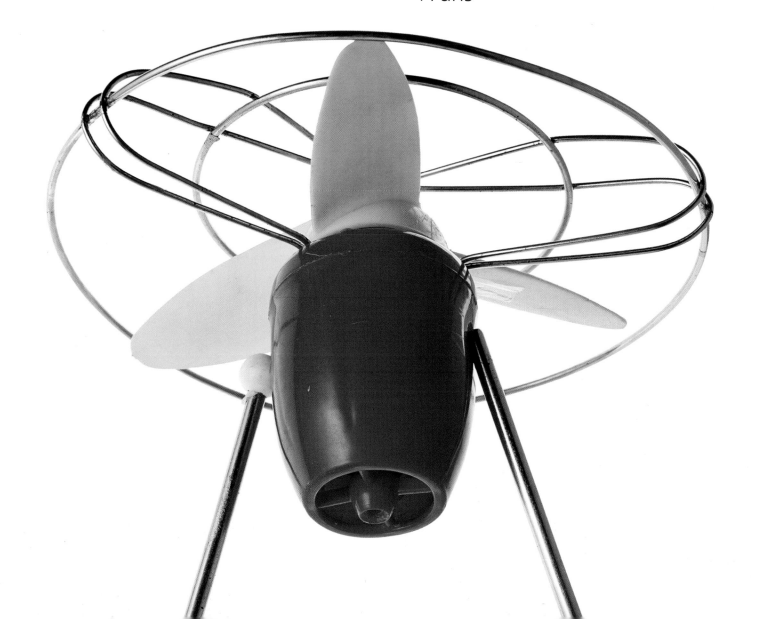

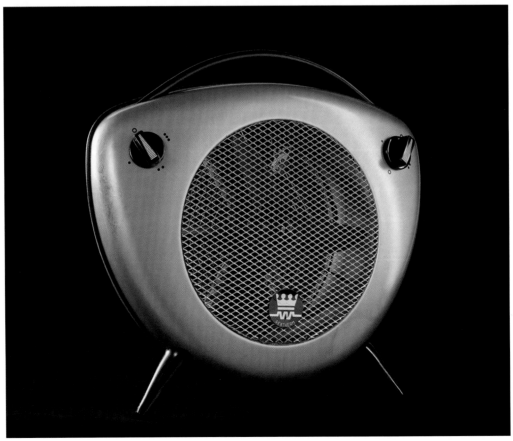

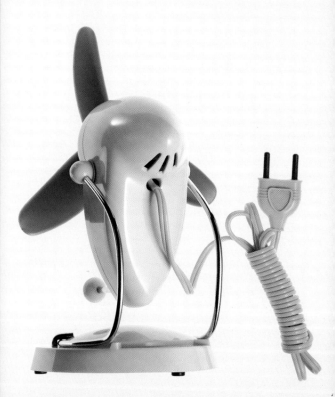

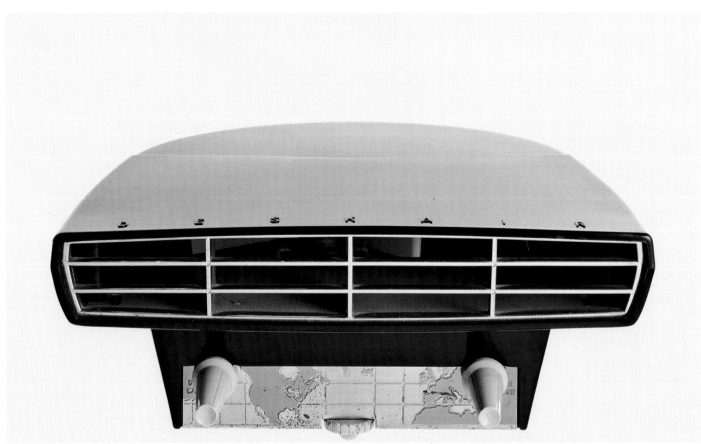

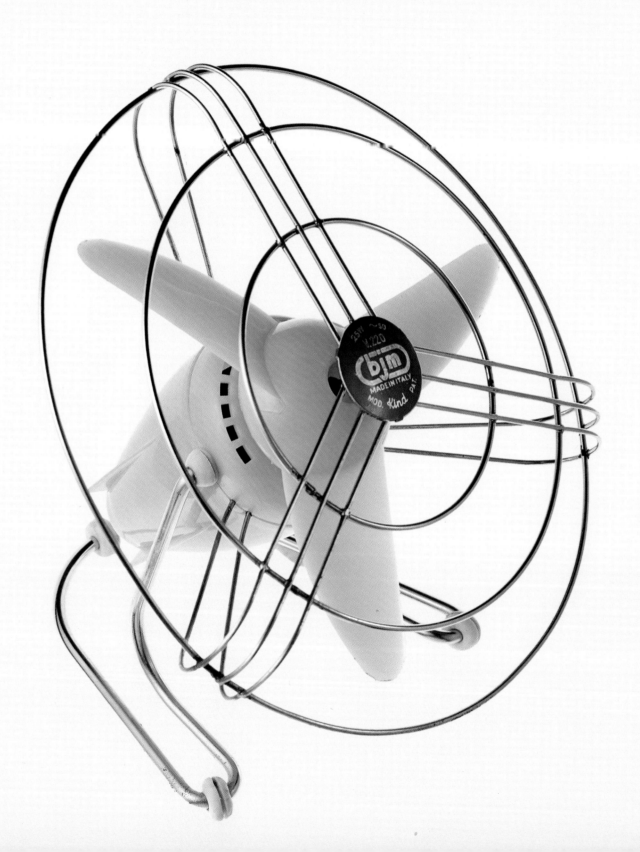

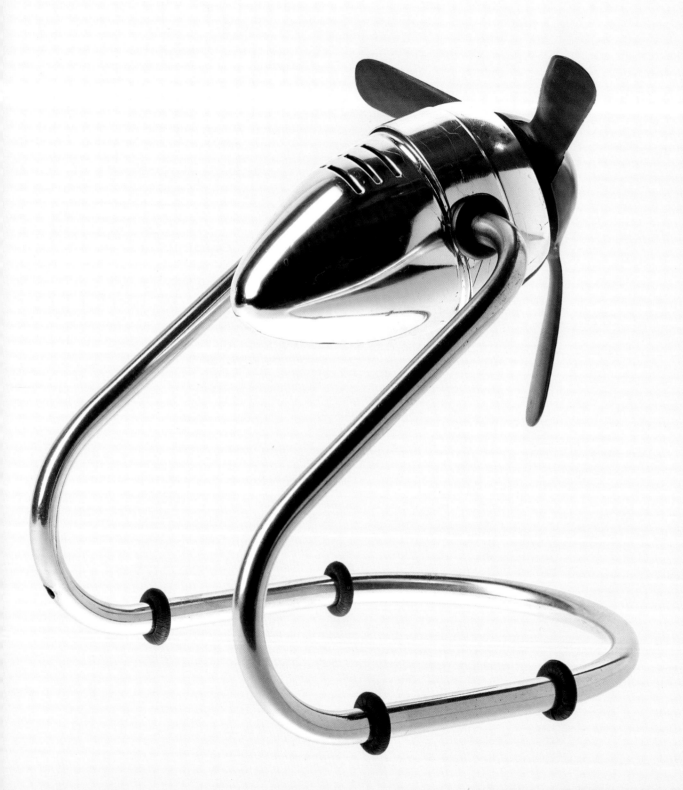

Washing

Cleansing

Vacuum Cleaners
Floor Polishers
Hair Dryers
Irons
Vibrators
UV Lamps
Bathroom Scales

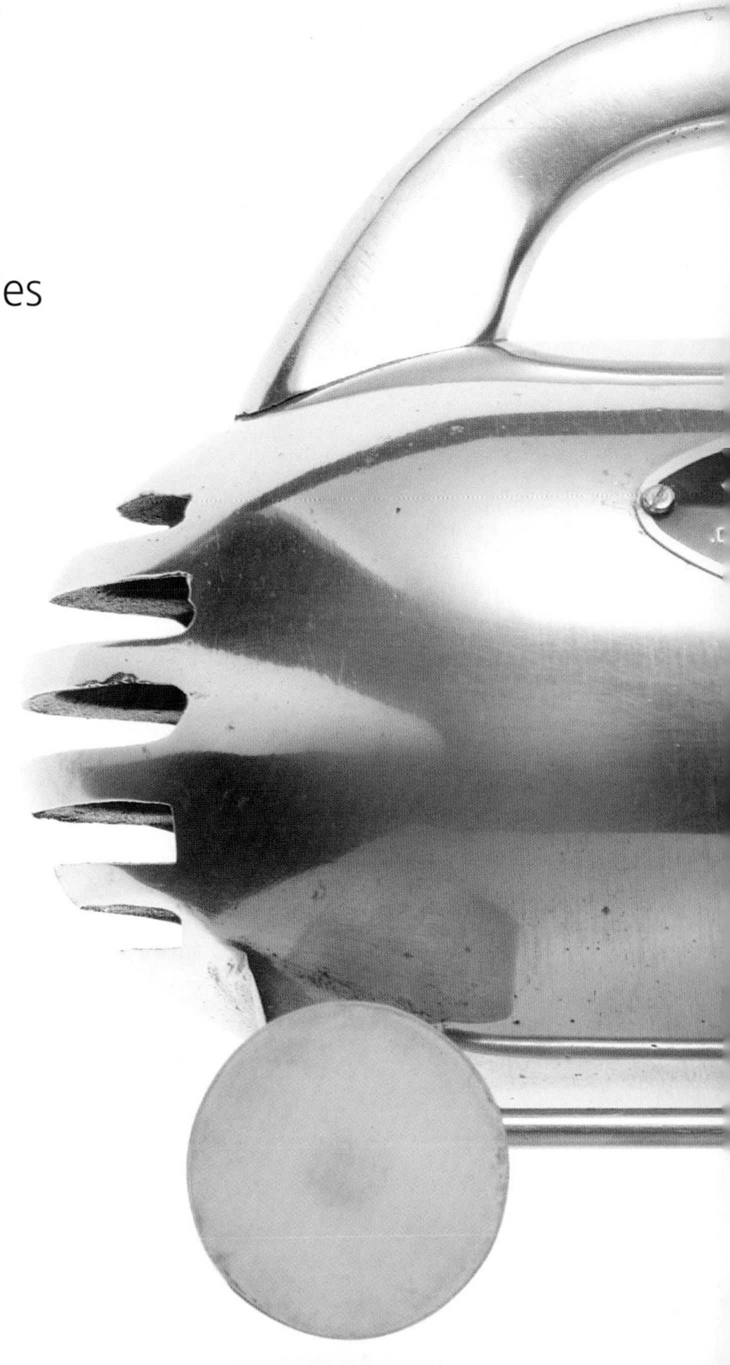

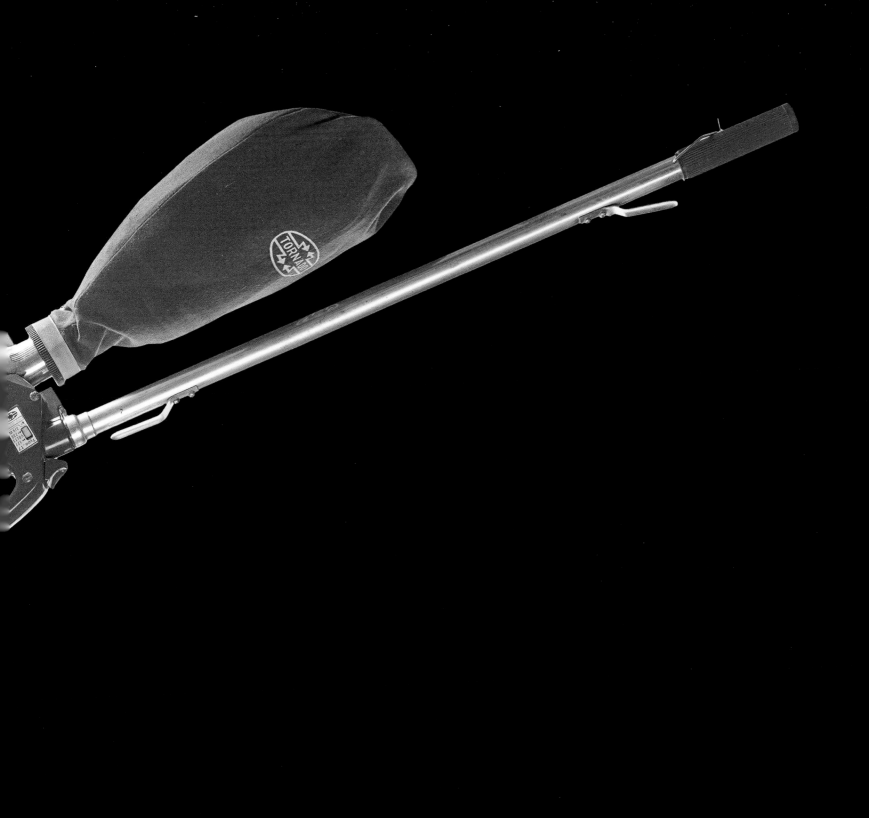

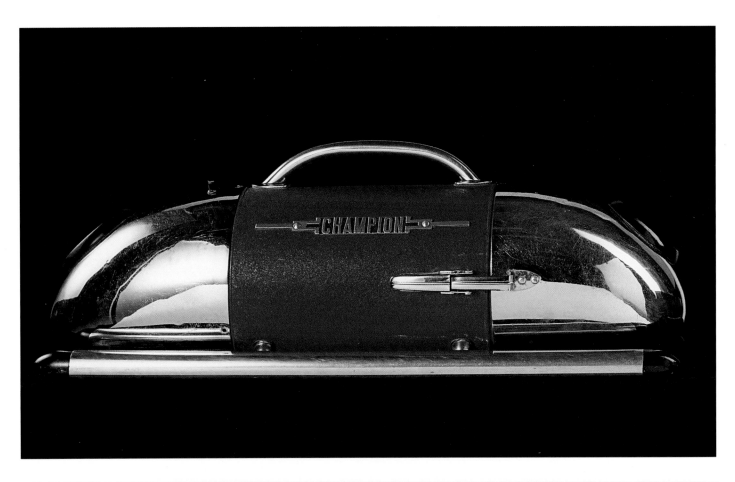

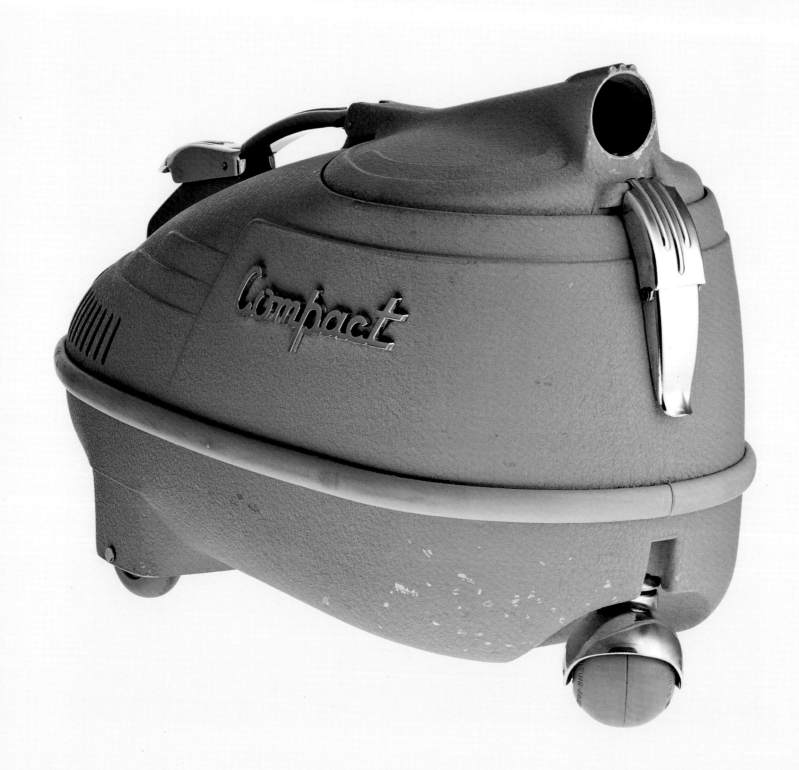

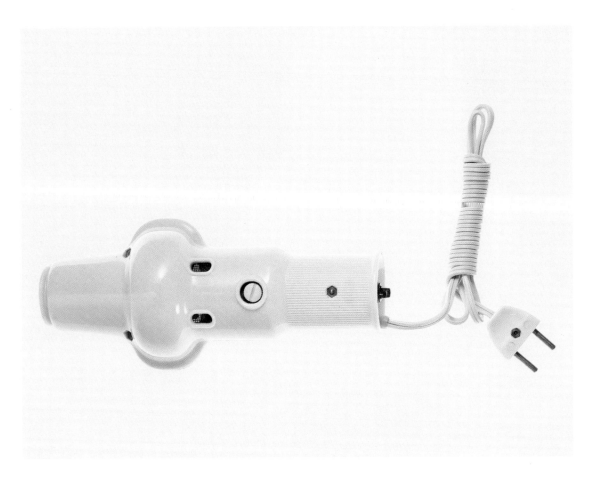

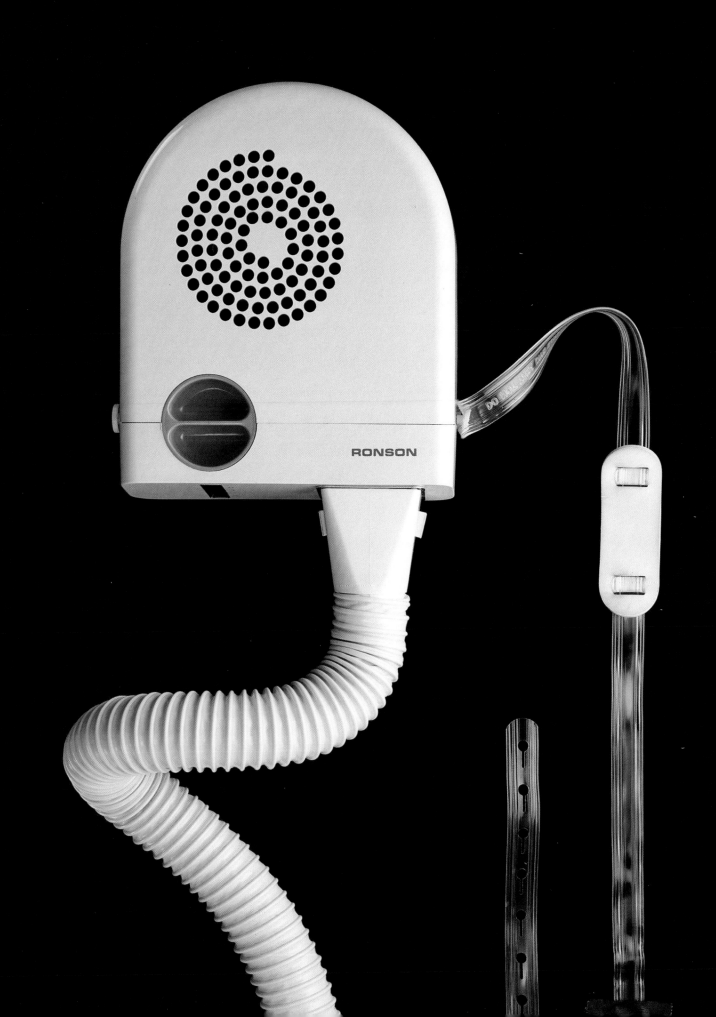

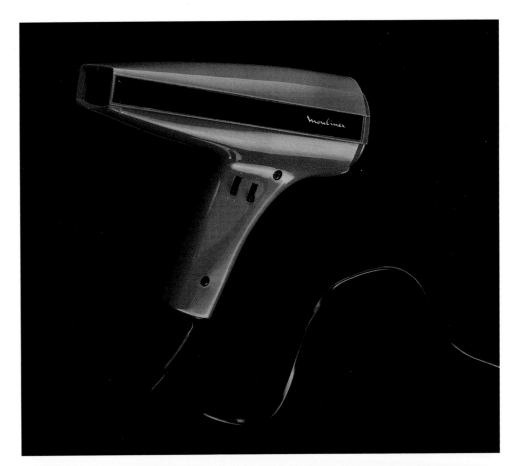

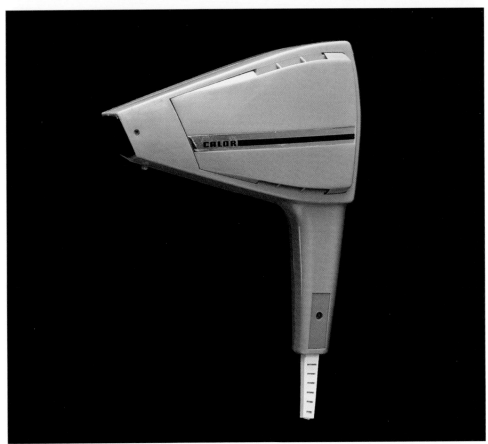

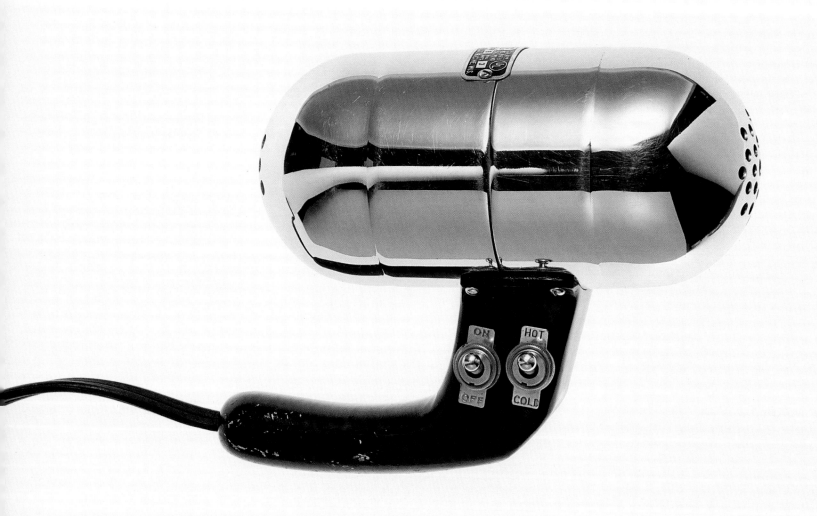

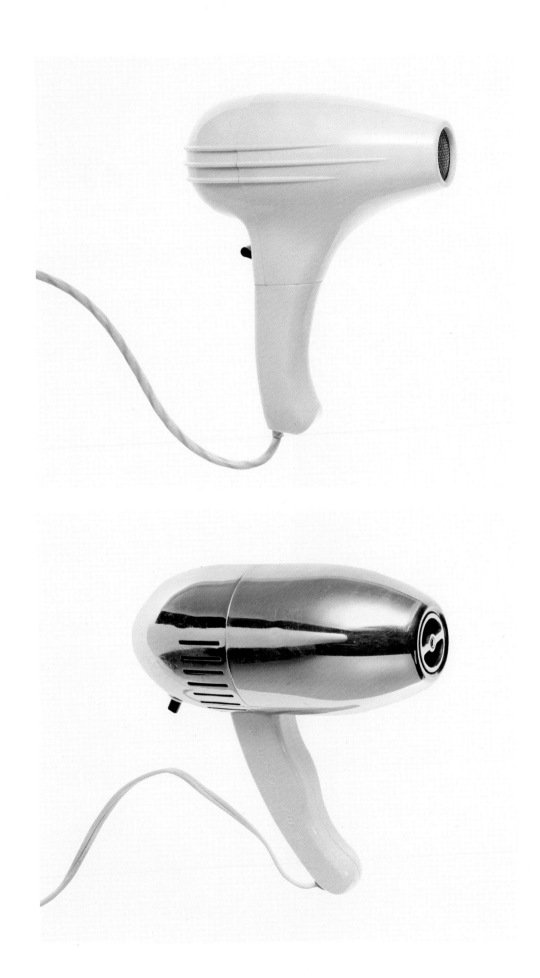

283

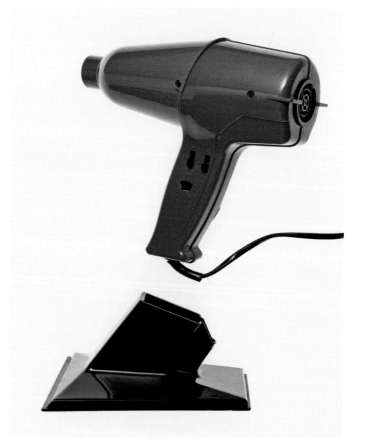

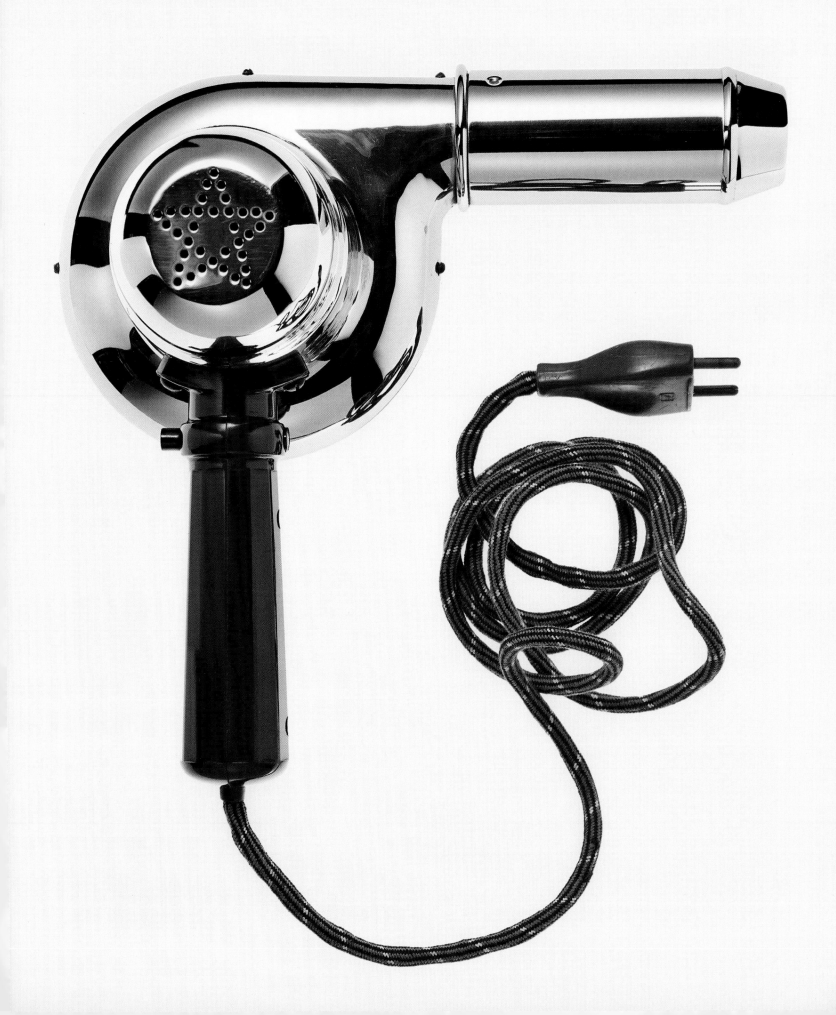

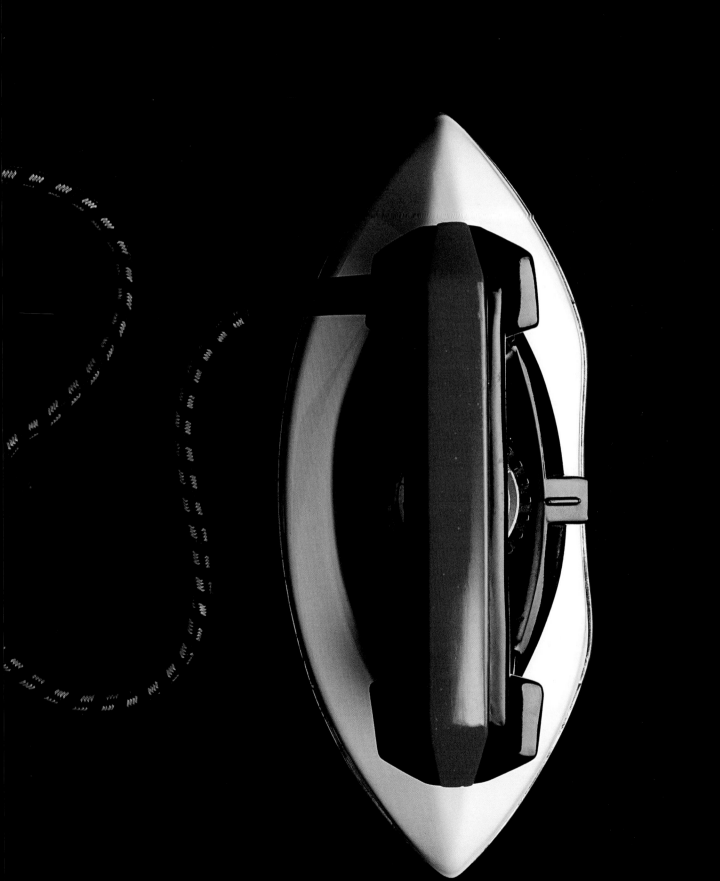

294

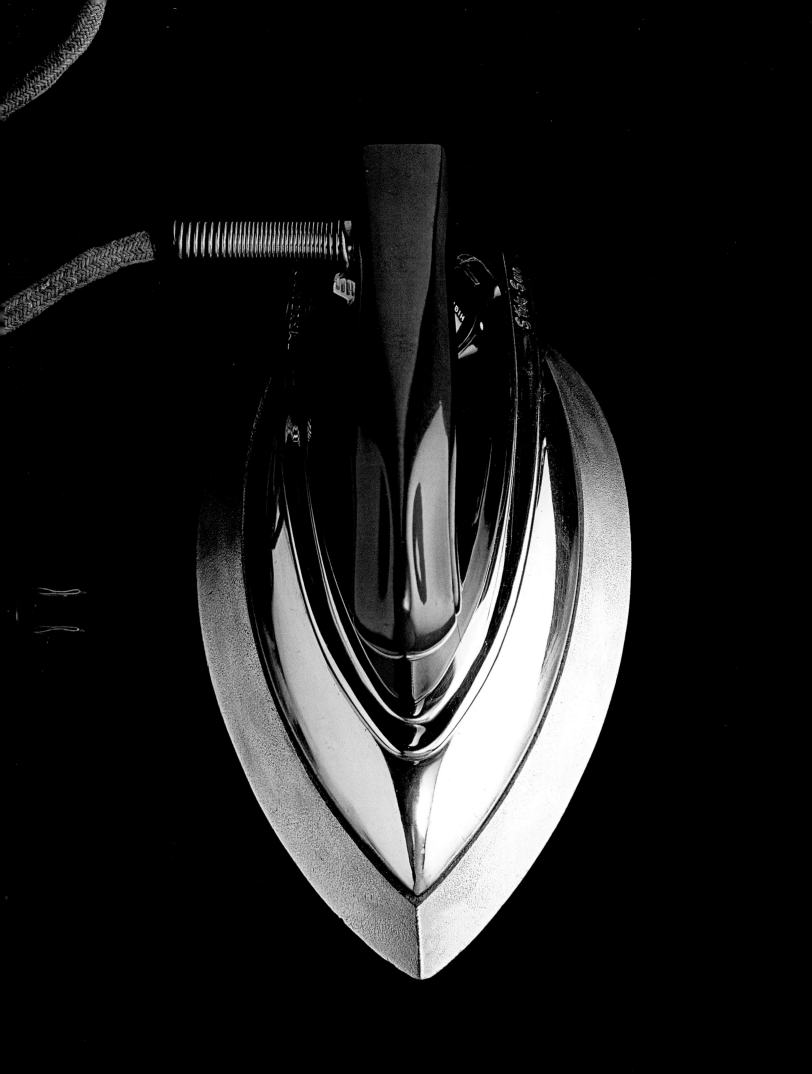

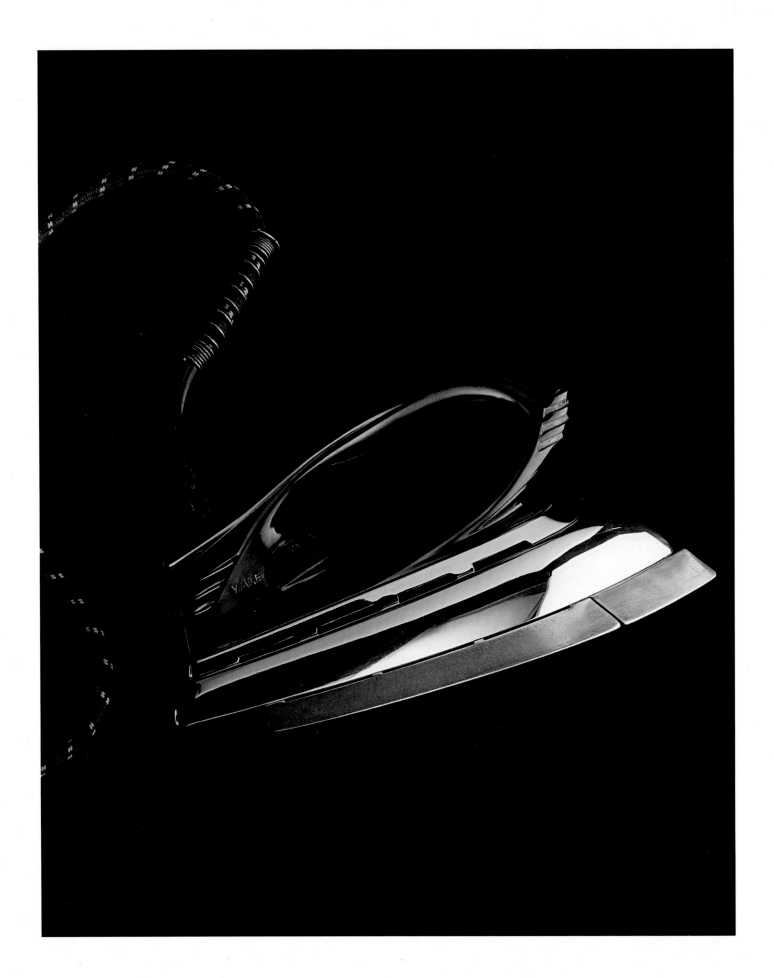

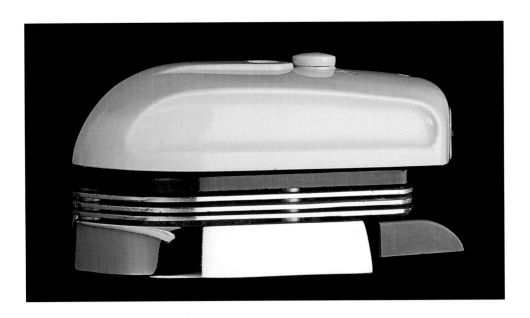

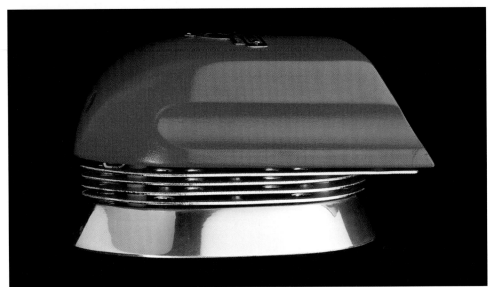

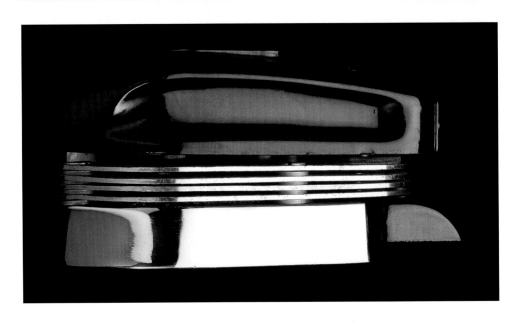

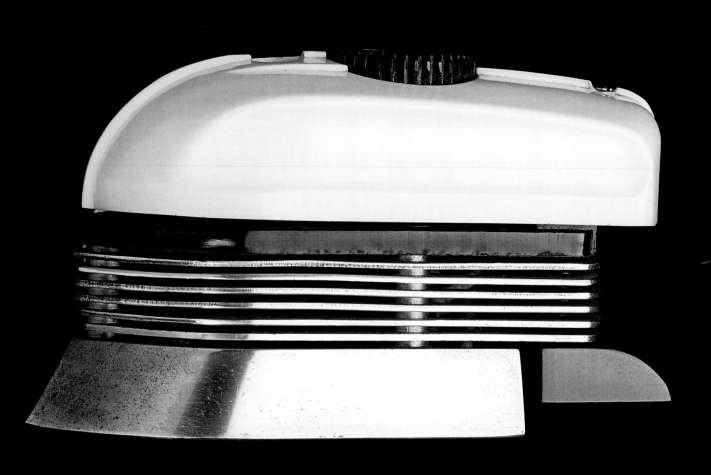

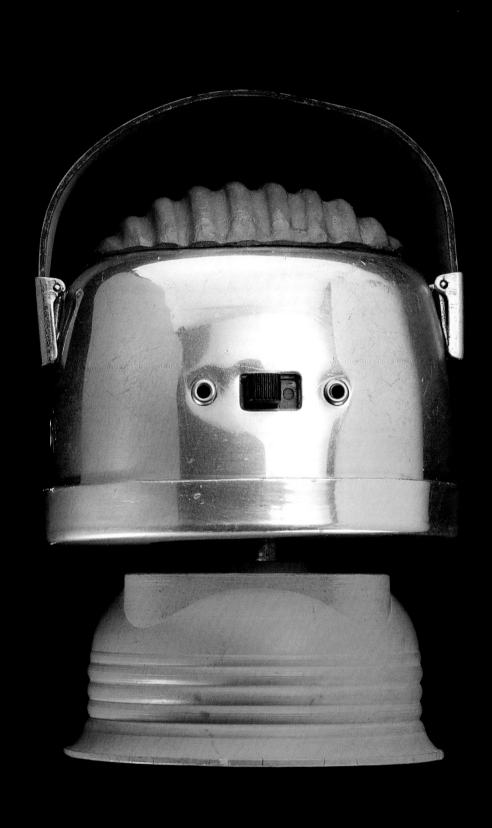

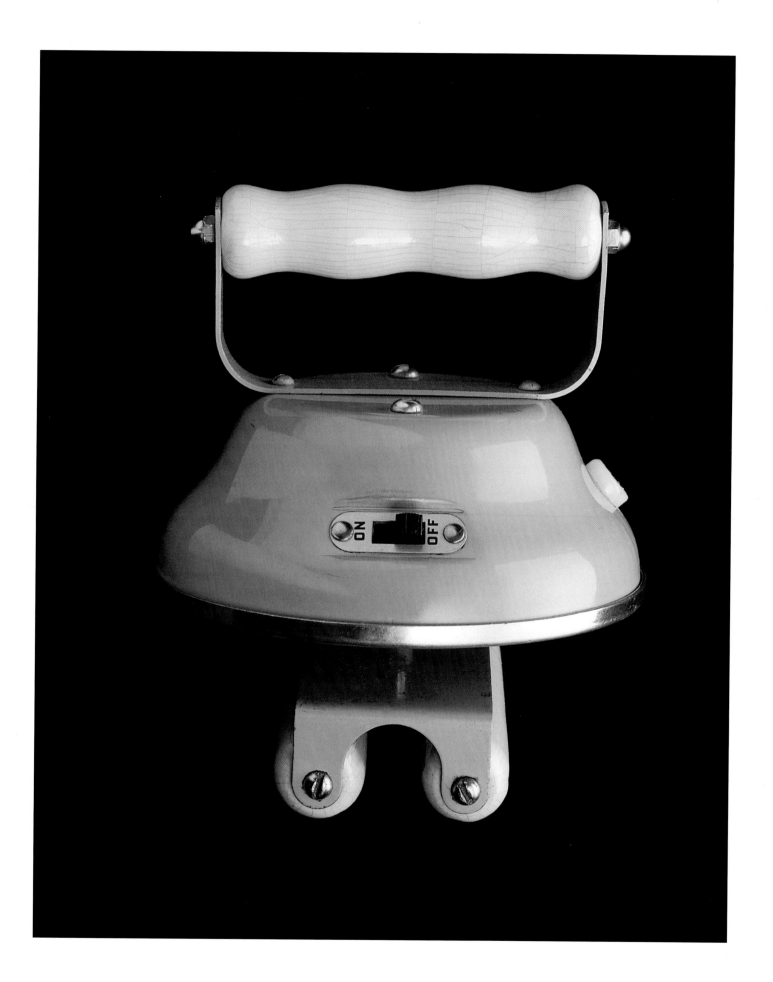

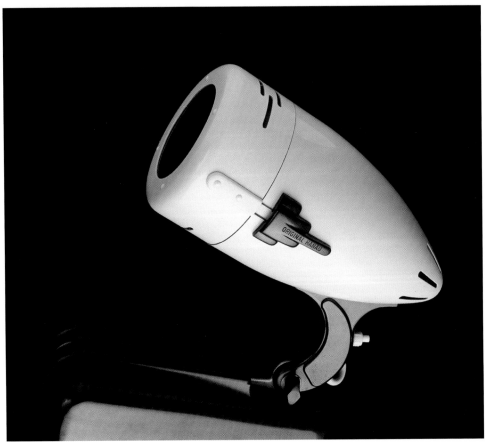

320

Sun-Kraft Jr.

REG. U.S. PAT. OFF.

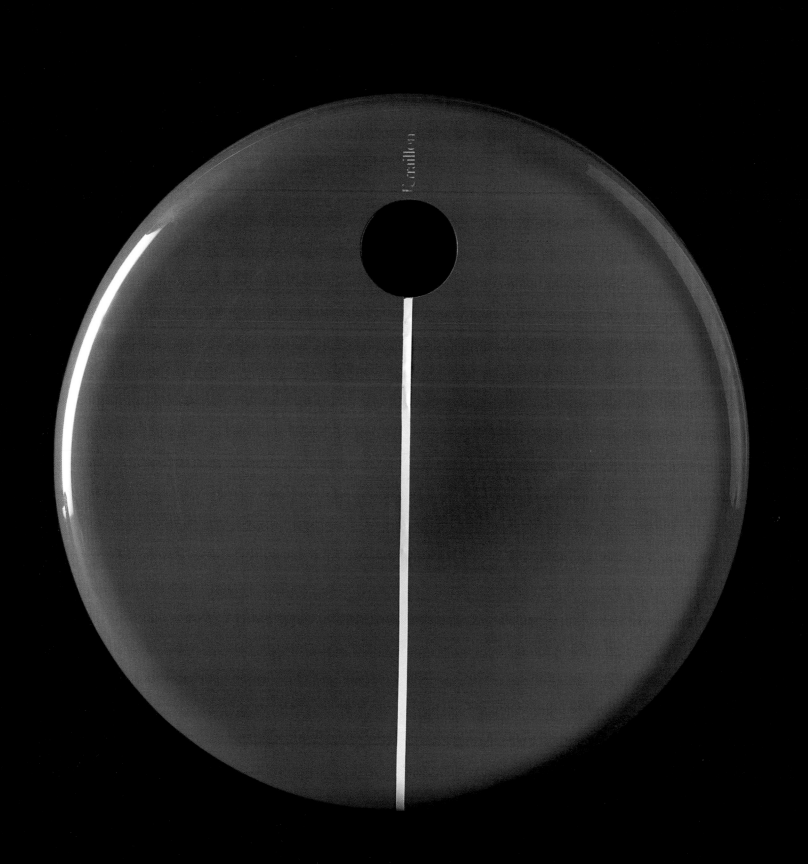

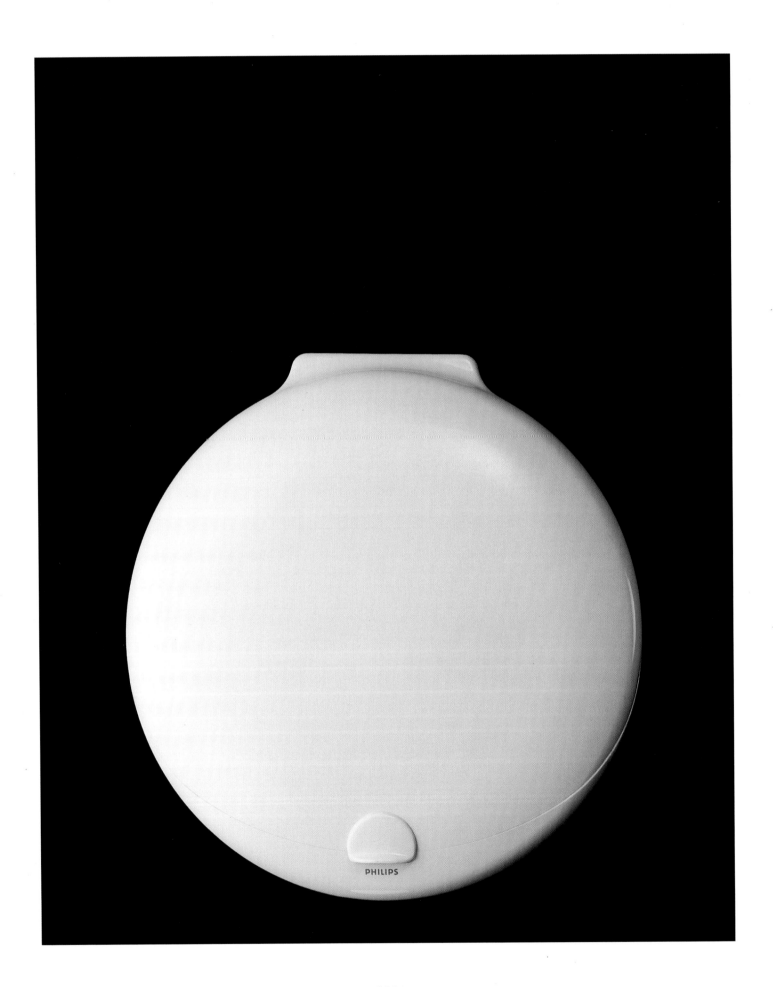

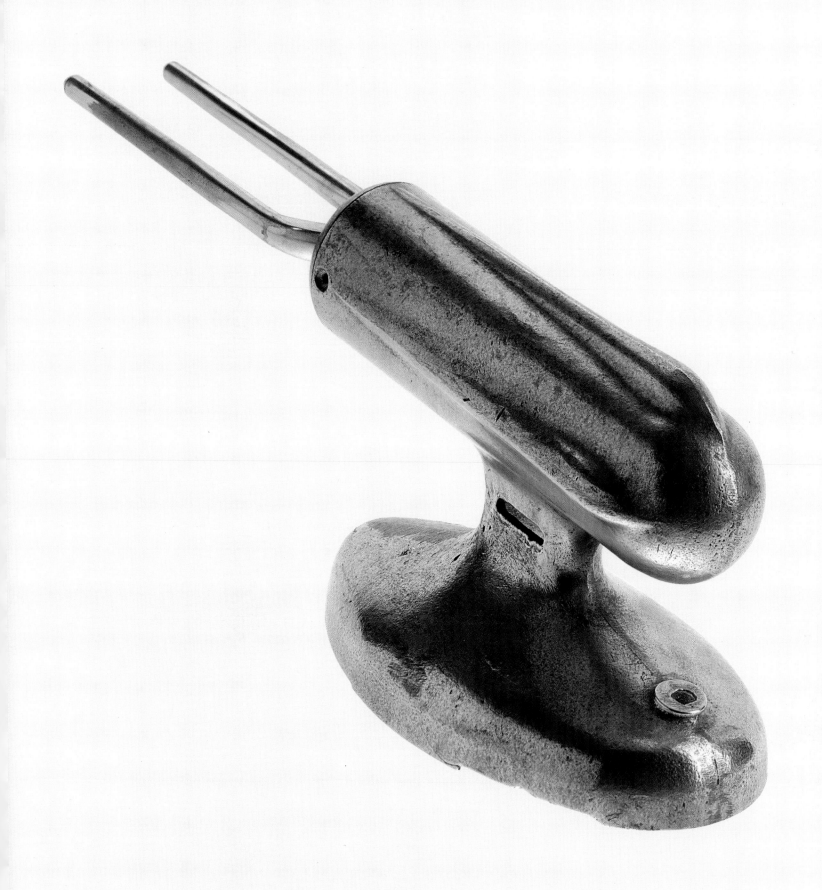

Author's Note

We researched all available sources, including websites and company archives in order to obtain the most basic information, namely:

- name of object
- year of manufacture
- city and country of origin
- manufacturer
- model
- designer(s)
- material(s)
- dimensions (cm)

The information we found was often contradictory:
- the year an object is registered frequently differs from the year it is marketed
- due to globalization, the year in which an object is marketed can often vary from country to country
- some designers do not take credit for certain designs. Manufacturers' archives are often "nonexistent" or very limited
- to the best of our knowledge, the information we have given is correct, particularly concerning dates, or at least years. This information was obtained by cross-checking several sources and relying on one of the few "truthful" sources : press ads (a company is unlikely to invest in an advertising campaign for an object which has not yet been marketed or which is no longer on the market).
Even so, a certain number of errors may have slipped into our captions. In the name of the sacrosanct *Errare humanun est, sed perseverare diabolicum*, we should be extremely grateful, firstly, if readers would be kind enough not to hold this against us and secondly, if they could share their expertise and sources with us so that we can correct any errors.
Likewise, if curious readers have any questions about objects in their possession or if they are able to provide us with any information, then they should not hesitate to contact us at: sumo3@wanadoo.fr.

List of Illustrations

Drinking | Eating

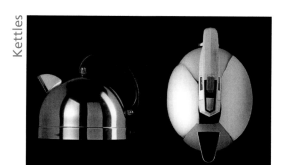

28-29

30-31

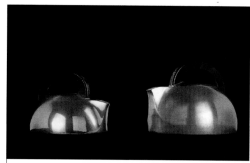

32-33

• Electric kettle
c. 1955 - Barrie, CAN
General Electric - K43B
Frederick Rowan
Chromed steel
and bakelite
21 x 21,5 x 24

• Electric kettle
c. 1955 - Barrie, CAN
General Electric - K60WC
Chromed steel
and melamine
22 x 19 x 26

• Kettle
c. 1938 - USA
Pure Aluminum
Sheet aluminum, painted
steel and painted wood
16 x 17,5 x 19

• Kettle
c. 1946 - USA
Sheet aluminum
and catalin
16 x 21 x 23

• Kettle
c. 1936 - USA
Sheet aluminum,
painted steel and bakelite
13 x 25 x 25

• Electric kettle
c. 1952 - Birmingham, UK
Swan Brand
Sheet aluminum
and bakelite
22 x 13 x 18

• Kettle
1940 - Sidney, AUS
Wagner Ware - Magnalite
Harold L. Van Doren
and John Gordon Rideout
Cast aluminum and
painted wood
18 x 22 x 23

• Kettle
c. 1940 - Sidney, AUS
Wagner Ware - Magnalite
Harold L. Van Doren
and John Gordon Rideout
Cast aluminum and wood
20 x 26 x 26

34-35

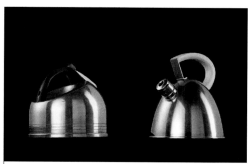

36-37

38-39

• Electric kettle
c. 1938 - Detroit, USA
Brannon
Hot-Water-Master
Polished cast aluminum,
chromed copper
and bakelite
22 x 22 x 23

• Kettle
c. 1938 - USA
Polished cast aluminum
and bakelite
20 x 25 x 25

• Kettle
c. 1947 - Chicago, USA
Ekco Products Co.
Whistler
Sheet aluminum
and bakelite
18 x 21 x 21

• Kettle
c. 1955 - D
Copper, stainless steel
and painted bakelite
22 x 20 x 20

• Kettle
1945 - Muncie, USA
Excel Mfg. Corp.
James H. Reichart
Sheet aluminum
and bakelite
26 x 24 x 24

• Kettle
c. 1945 - USA
Guardian Service
Hammered cast iron
and bakelite
24 x 19 x 26

Ice crushers

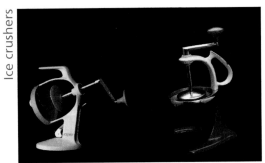

40-41

42-43

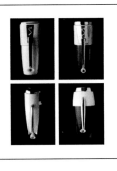

44-45

• Ice rasp
c. 1962 - JPN
Fuso Keigokin K-K - Icepet
*Painted zamac, steel
and polystyrene
20 x 11 x 24*

• Ice rasp
c. 1950 - USA
*Painted cast iron, cast
aluminum, polystyrene
and sheet aluminum
28 x 16 x 16*

• Ice crushers (1 - 2)
1954 - Kansas City, USA
Rival - Ice-O-Mat wall
Model "Bucketter" - NK480
Sheldon M. Rutter
(1) *Chromed zamac,
chromed brass
and polystyrene
22 x 13 x 19*
(2) *Chromed zamac
and chromed brass
23 x 14 x 19*

• Ice crushers (3 - 4)
1960 - Kansas City, USA
Rival - Ice-O-Mat Deluxe
Ice Crusher - TW347
Sheldon M. Rutter
*Painted zamac, chromed
zamac and polypropylene
24 x 11,5 x 14*

• Ice crusher (5)
c. 1945 - Saint Louis, USA
Dazey - 160
Jean Otis Reinecke
*Painted zamac
and polystyrene
31 x 13 x 19*

• Ice crushers (1 - 2)
1954 - Saint Louis, USA
Dazey - Swing-A-Way
Walter E. Moore
(1) *Chromed zamac,
painted zamac and high
density polyethylene
22,5 x 8 x 17*
(2) *Chromed zamac,
painted zamac and
polystyrene - 22,5 x 8 x 16*

• Ice crusher (3)
c. 1945 - Saint Louis, USA
Dazey
Jean Otis Reinecke

*Painted zamac, chromed
zamac and polystyrene
24,5 x 9 x 15*

• Ice crusher (4)
c. 1950 - Saint Louis, USA
Dazey - Iceramic
*Chromed zamac, painted
zamac, polystyrene and
cork - 26 x 11 x 17*

• Ice crusher (5)
c. 1954 - Kansas City, USA
Magic Hostess - 542
*Chromed zamac and
polystyrene - 23 x 10 x 15*

46-47

48-49

50-51

• Ice crusher
1940 - Chicago, USA
Die Casting Mfg. Co.
Ice Flow
William P. Koch
*Painted zamac
17 x 14 x 24*

• Ice crusher
1934 - Chicago, USA
National - Ice-Crusher
Herbert C. Johnson
*Painted zamac
and painted wood
23 x 18 x 13*

• Ice crusher
1939 - Kansas City, USA
Rival - Ice-O-Mat
Joseph M. Majewski Jr
*Chromed zamac
and painted zamac
25 x 14,5 x 14*

• Ice crusher
c. 1940 - Los Angeles, USA
Opco - The Ice-Gun
*Painted zamac
and chromed steel
16 x 27 x 16*

Centrifugal machines

Blenders

52-53

54-55

56-57

- **Blender**
1947 - Küsnacht, CH
Techag A.G. - Turmix 4
Chromed sheet steel,
glass and sheet aluminum
48 x 16 x 17

- **Blender with juicer**
1947 - Küsnacht, CH
Techag A.G. - Turmix 4
Chromed sheet steel
and cast aluminum
45 x 21 x 21

- **Centrifugal machine**
1952 - Frankfurt, D
Braun - Multipress
Artur & Erwin Braun
Bakelite, polystyrene,
rubber and chromed steel
28 x 18 x 19

- **Centrifugal machine**
1970 - Frankfurt, D
Braun - Multipress - MP50
Jürgen Greubel
ABS and chromed steel
28 x 22 x 20

- **Centrifugal machine**
c. 1954 - CH
Ellis - Super
Polystyrene, high density
polyethylene and steel
34 x 21 x 19

- **Centrifugal machine**
1960 - D
Novalux - 11-09
H. Ehring
Melamine
21 x 17 x 19

- **Blender**
1947 - Küsnacht, CH
Techag A.G. - Turmix 4
Chromed sheet steel,
and cast aluminum
47 x 16 x 17

- **Blender-mixer**
1947 - Küsnacht, CH
Techag A.G. - Turmix 4
Chromed sheet steel,
glass, cast aluminum
and bakelite
50 x 23 x 23

58-59

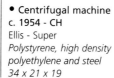

60-61

62-63

- **Blender**
c. 1959 - Los Angeles, USA
Castman & Weiss Dist. Co.
Blender Queen - NBC
Henry A. Dewenter
(technician)
Bakelite coated with a
sheet of chromed steel,
stainless steel, chromed
zamac and polystyrene
39 x 15 x 18

- **Blender**
c. 1954 - Chicago, USA
Kenmore - 116-82 421
Painted zamac, glass,
bakelite and rubber
32 x 18 x 18

- **Blender**
c. 1950 - Küsnacht, CH
Techag A.G. - Turmix AV
Bakelite and glass
42 x 18 x 18

- **Blender**
1955 - Prague, CZ
Kovotechna - Pragomix
Milos Hajek
Painted cast aluminum,
glass, bakelite and high
density polyethylene
42 x 17 x 17

- **Blender**
c. 1950 - I
Vosta - Berolina
Painted steel, glass,
polystyrene, polyethylene,
rubber and polished
aluminum
46 x 18 x 20

- **Blender**
c. 1954 - Chicago, USA
Dormeyer
Blend Well BL - 2 PK
Polystyrene and
chromed zamac
40 x 20 x 20

Blenders

64-65

66-67

68-69

● Blender
1941 - Glendale, USA
Hollywood Liquifier Corp.
Blender Queen n° 41
Don E. Grove
*Melamine and methyl
polyacrylate*
36 x 12 x 21

● Blender
1956 - New York, USA
Waring Product Corp.
Waring Blendor + Ice Jet
Frederic J. Osius
(designer and technician)
*Chromed zamac, painted
zamac and polyethylene*
40 x 17 x 24

● Blender
c. 1950 - Frankfurt, D
Braun - M2
Max Braun
*Bakelite, glass and
polished and turned
cast aluminum*
43 x 15 x 15

● Blender
c. 1950 - Frankfurt, D
Braun - M2
Max Braun
*Bakelite, glass and
polished and turned
cast aluminum*
43 x 15 x 15

● Blender
c. 1960 - Tokyo, JPN
Mitsubishi Electric
JM 802
*Painted steel, chromed
steel, glass, melamine
and polyethylene*
42 x 20 x 21

● Blender
c. 1956 - Milwaukee, USA
John Oster Mfg. Co.
Osterizer Deluxe - 403
and accessory - 433 B
Stefen J. Poblawski
*Chromed zamac, cellulose
acetate, steel and zamac*
36 x 27 x 17

Juicers

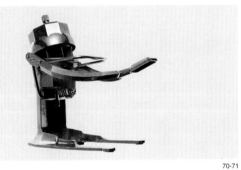

70-71

72-73

74-75

● Juicer
c. 1978 - F
SEB - 305
*ABS and methyl
polyacrylate*
13 x 15 x 15

● Juicer
c. 1935 - New York, USA
Royal Aluminum Corp.
Whole Fruit
*Polished cast aluminum
and chromed copper*
34 x 17 x 35

● Juicer
c. 1976 - Alençon, F
Moulinex - 138601
Jean-Louis Barrault
ABS and acrylic
20 x 30 x 30

● Juicer
c. 1957 - F
Plastiva
Low density polyethylene
10 x 19 x 14

● Juicer
c. 1945 - Saint Louis, USA
Dazey - Speedo-Juicer
*Polished cast aluminum,
sheet aluminum and wood*
14 x 13 x 14

● Juicer
1941 - Kansas City, USA
Rival - Juice-o-Mat
Wall Type
Joseph M. Majewski Jr.
*Polished cast aluminum
and cellulose acetate*
17 x 16 x 13

Drinking Eating

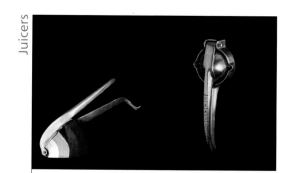

76-77

78-79

80-81

• Juicer
c. 1950 - I
Mondial
Polished cast aluminum
18 x 11 x 25

• Juicer
c. 1950 - Rockford, USA
Ebaloy Inc.
Unwrought cast
aluminum
6 x 13 x 33

• Juicer
c. 1950 - Turin, I
D. Rasero & Co.
Painted zamac and
polished cast aluminum
21 x 18 x 20

• Juicer
c. 1970 - I
SRC
High density polyethylene,
chromed steel
and elastomer
24 x 15 x 27

• Hand juicer
c. 1950 - Boston, USA
L. E. Mason
Unwrought cast
aluminum and polished
cast aluminum
22 x 20 x 18

• Juicer
c. 1936 - USA
The Big Squeeze
Polished cast aluminum
24 x 13 x 22

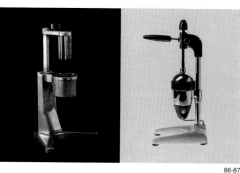

82-83

84-85

86-87

• Juicer
c. 1946 - Chicago, USA
National Die Casting Co.
Juice King - JK-40
Chromed zamac, painted
zamac, polished cast
aluminum and ebonite
28 x 21 x 21

• Juicer
c. 1946 - Chicago, USA
National Die Casting Co.
Juice King - JK-50
Chromed zamac, cast
aluminum and ebonite
26 x 18 x 21

• Juicer
c. 1976 - UK
High density polyethylene
and galvanised steel
26 x 15 x 31

• Juicer
1945 - Kansas City, USA
Rival - Juice-O-Mat
"Tilt-Top" - A648
Joseph M. Majewski Jr.
& Henry J. Talge. Albert E.
Grant (technician)
Chromed zamac and
polished cast aluminum
22 x 17 x 20

• Lemon sectionizer
c. 1938 - USA
Sunkist
Zamac, sheet steel,
brass and rubber
43 x 30 x 20

• Juicer
1939 - Racine, USA
Hamilton Beach
James F. Barnes and
Jean Otis Reinecke
Enamelled cast iron,
chromed cast iron, painted
cast iron, chromed zamac,
rubber and bakelite
51 x 18 x 23

88-89

90-91

92-93

• Juicer
1948 - Kansas City, USA
Rival - Juice-O-Mat Deluxe
"Tilt Top"
Elton F. Whitfill
and Henry J.Talge
*Chromed zamac and
polished cast aluminum
16 x 16 x 16*

• Bar juicer
c. 1970 - Milano, I
Vema
*Polished cast aluminum,
sheet aluminum, stainless
steel and polycarbonate
33 x 27 x 18*

• Electric bar juicer
c. 1960 - Los Angeles, USA
Sunkist Growers Inc - 6
*Chromed steel, stainless
steel and cast aluminum
lined with stainless steel
45 x 23 x 17*

• Juicer
c. 1940 - I
Alpro Sa
*Polished or painted zamac
50 x 25 x 25*

• Juicer
c. 1940 - USA
Anonymous
*Polished or painted
cast aluminum
54 x 20 x 46*

94-95

96-97

98-99

Electric coffee mills

• c. 1957 - Europe
Molex
*Polystyrene, glass and
polyethylene - 16 x 9 x 9*

• c. 1952 - Leipzig, D
Galvanotechnik - Pirouette P3
Melamine, glass - 15 x 10 x 10

• 1960 - Eindhoven, NL
Philips - HM 3210
*Polyproylene and
polystyrene - 16 x 10 x 9*

• c. 1955 - F
*Polystyrene, melamine,
zamac, rubber - 12 x 12 x 12*

• c. 1958 - CH
Mivit 7660
*Polyproylene and
polystyrene - 16 x 8 x 10*

• 1960 - Alençon, F
Moulinex - Junior
Roger Georges (technician)
*Polystyrene, lacquered
steel and rubber
15 x 8,5 x 8,5*

• c. 1965 - Omegna, I
La Subalpina - Girmi
Macinacaffè Major
Polystyrene, PVC - 13 x 11 x 11

• Electric coffee mill
c.1952 - Iserlohn, D
K.Y.M. - Elenova
*Painted cast aluminum,
bakelite, polystyrene
and rubber
17 x 9 x 24*

• Coffee mill
c. 1950 - F
Hop
*Sheet aluminum,
steel and painted wood
18 x 9 x 15*

• Coffee mill
c. 1948 - F
Moulux
*Partially polished cast
aluminum and wood
9 x 19 x 13*

• Electric coffee mill
1949 - Paris, F
S.E.V - 50
*Glass and painted zamac
31 x 12 x 13*

Coffee mills

100-101

102-103

104-105

• Coffee mill
1947 - Kansas City, USA
Rival
Henry J. Talge
and Albert M. Travis
Chromed zamac,
acrylic and painted wood
22 x 22 x 9

• Electric coffee mill
c. 1955 - F
Mistral - Universal
Chromed steel
and polystyrene
21 x 11 x 11

• Electric coffee mill
1954 - Frankfurt, D
A.E.G - KME6
Hans Krebs
Polystyrene
16 x 10 x 20

• Electric coffee mill
c. 1959 - Frankfurt, D
A.E.G – KMU
Peter Sieberg
Polystyrene
16 x 10 x 15

• Electric coffee mills
c. 1967 - Frankfurt, D
Braun - KSM 1/11
Reinhold Weiss
ABS
17 x 8 x 8

• Electric coffee mill
c. 1960 - Schwenningen, D
G. Widmann & Söhne,
KG - Wigo Plus
John E. Knox
ABS, acrylic
and sheet aluminum
18 x 10 x 10

Coffee makers

106-107

108-109

110-111

• Electric coffee mill
c. 1975 - Liège, B
Kalorik - 5422
ABS and methyl
polyacrylate
19 x 10 x 19

• Electric coffee mill
c. 1953 - Dole, F
Kerry
Polystyrene and bakelite
13 x 13 x 21

• Coffee maker
c. 1950 - I
Trimmel
Cast aluminum
and bakelite
20 x 20 x 26

• Coffee maker
c. 1950 - n.p.
Cast and sheet aluminum
and bakelite
28 x 16 x 30

• Coffee maker
1932 - New Kensington,
USA
The Aluminum Cooking
Utensil Co. - Wear-Ever
5052
Lurelle Guild
Sheet aluminum
and bakelite
28 x 23 x 11

• Coffee maker
c. 1950 - USA
West Bend Aluminum Co.
Kwik Drip
Sheet aluminum
and bakelite
37 x 18 x 27

Coffee makers

112-113

114-115

116-117

● Coffee maker
c. 1960 - CH
Therma - 3321
Chromed steel
34 x 18 x 20

● Electric coffee maker
1954 - D
Patzner K G - Palux
Nickel-plated cast
aluminum, polished cast
aluminum, nickel-plated
brass, nickel-plated
steel and bakelite
38 x 17 x 17

● Electric coffee maker
c. 1950 - I
Caravel
Painted cast aluminum
and stainless steel
32 x 18 x 30

● Coffee maker
c. 1960 - I
La Signora
Cast aluminum
and bakelite
27 x 12 x 20

● Coffee maker
1947 - Milan, I
Atomic
Polished cast aluminum,
bakelite and chromed
copper
21 x 26 x 15

● Coffee maker
c. 1955 - Binasco, I
Faema - Baby Faemina
Polished and painted
cast aluminum
50 x 18 x 18

● Coffee maker
1958 - Milan, I
Diana
Emanuele Zigomalas
Chromed steel
and polyethylene
47 x 40 x 16

Pitchers

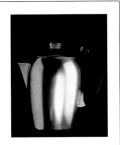

118-119

120-121

122-123

● Coffee maker
1947 - Chicago, USA
Cory - DIU
Harper Richards
Toughened glass,
bakelite and melamine
34 x 21 x 16

● Electric coffee maker
c. 1949 - Chicago, USA
Cory - ACB-2
Chromed steel
and bakelite
30 x 22 x 16

● Kettle
1943 - Chicago, USA
Club Aluminum
Products Co.
Dave Chapman
Toughened glass
and bakelite
20 x 20 x 16

● Serving pitcher
c. 1938 - New
Kensington, USA
Kensington - 7730
Lurelle Guild
Sheet aluminum, bakelite
and cast aluminum
20 x 20 x 13

● Coffee maker
c. 1938 - New
Kensington, USA
The Aluminum Cooking
Utensil Co. - Wear Ever
Hallite - 3088
Lurelle Guild
Aluminum, bakelite
and glass
21 x 21 x 15

Pitchers

124-125

126-127

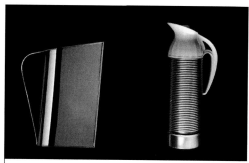

128-129

• Thermos pitcher
and tray
1935 - Norwitch, USA
The American Thermos
Bottle Co. - 539
Henry Dreyfuss
*Painted sheet aluminum,
chromed zamac, glass and
painted sheet steel (tray)*
15 x 10 x 14
(tray: 2 x 23 x 17)

• Thermos pitcher
and tray
1935 - Norwitch, USA
The American Thermos
Bottle Co. - 539
Henry Dreyfuss
*Painted sheet aluminum,
chromed zamac, glass and
painted sheet steel (tray)*
15 x 10 x 14
(tray: 2 x 23 x 17)

• Thermos pitcher
c. 1930 - Meriden, USA
Manning-Bowman
*Painted brass, chromed
brass and glass*
24 x 18 x 13

• Thermos pitcher
c. 1930 - New Britain, USA
Landers Frary & Clark/
Universal
*Painted brass, stainless
steel, chromed zamac
and glass*
19,5 x 14 x 11

• Pitcher
c. 1935 - USA
Pitcher - Kromex
*Sheet aluminum
and bakelite*
18,5 x 18 x 14

• Pitcher
c. 1935 - New York, USA
Revere Copper and Brass
Inc. - Normandie
Peter Müller - Munk
Chromed brass
30,5 x 24 x 7,3

• Thermos bottle
c. 1938 - CH
Theos
*Painted sheet aluminum
and polystyrene*
28,5 x 13 x 9

130-131

132-133

Food processors

134-135

• Thermos pitcher
c. 1938 - Meriden, USA
Manning-Bowman
*Chromed copper,
painted copper
and chromed zamac*
19 x 19 x 15

• Coffee pot
c. 1925 - Chicago, USA
Club Aluminum Ware
with Personal Service - M
*Cast aluminum
and painted wood*
28 x 22 x 16

• Orangeade pitcher
1932 - New York, USA
Wright Accessories
Russel Wright
*Brushed sheet aluminum
and wood*
26 x 27 x 15

• Food processor
1950 - Troy, USA
4C
Egmont Arens
*Painted zamac
and stainless steel*
35 x 19 x 30

• Food processor
1940 - Racine, USA
Hamilton Beach - E
Zamac, steel and bakelite
35 x 19 x 52

Food processors

136-137

138-139

140-141

Beaters

• c. 1960 - Chicago, USA
Sunbeam - Mixmaster HM-1
*Cellulose acetate, painted
zamac, embossed sheet
aluminum and chromed
steel - 24 x 8 x 19*

• c. 1960 - New York, USA
Waring - RM2 Mixor
*Cellulose acetate, painted
zamac, chromed steel and
neoprene - 28 x 7 x 18*

• c. 1960 - Mansfield, USA
Westinghouse - HM9A-1

*Cellulose acetate, painted
zamac and chromed steel
27 x 8,5 x 20*

• c. 1960 - Bridgeport, USA
General Electric
*Cellulose acetate,
neoprene, aluminum
and chromed steel
25 x 9,5 x 22*

• 1955 - Chicago, USA
Sunbeam - Mixmaster
Junior
Ivar Jepson
*Chromed zamac, bakelite,
stainless steel - 26 x16 x 8*

• **Hand beater**
1915 - New York, USA
United Royalties Corp.
Ladd Beater n°1
*Nickel-plated steel
31 x 8,5 x 11*

• **Beater**
c. 1958 - Brussels, B
Kalorik - Mixette
*Cellulose acetate
and polyamide
27 x 7 x 19*

• **Hand beater**
c. 1960 - I
Manomix
*Melamine, polystyrene,
wood, chromed steel
and aluminum
27 x 18 x 28*

• **Plunger**
c. 1958 - B
Magic Belgium
*Melamine and polished
cast aluminum
38 x 9 x 19*

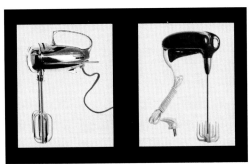

142-143

144-145

Shakers and siphons

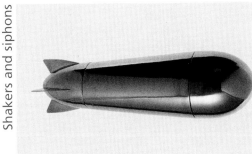

146-147

• **Beater**
c. 1955 - Manchester, USA
The Iona Mfg. Co.
Regent - 12P
*Chromed zamac
and chromed steel
27 x 7 x 16*

• **Beater**
c. 1953 - n.p.
*Bakelite, chromed steel,
polished cast aluminum
and polyamide
27 x 6 x 15*

• **Food processor**
1952 - Boonville, USA
Mc Graw Elec. Co.
GM - 7A
Howard H. Scott
*Chromed zamac,
chromed steel and bakelite
32 x 19 x 30*

• **Food processor**
1957 - Chicago, USA
Sunbeam
Mixmaster - 11C
Ivar Jepson
*Chromed zamac,
bakelite, chromed steel,
toughened glass, ceramic
and stainless steel
38 x 19 x 30*

• **Cocktail service**
c. 1925 - D
*Nickel-plated brass
30 x 9 x 9*

Shakers and siphons

148-149

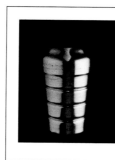

150-151

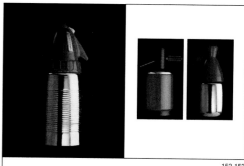

152-153

• Whipped cream
siphon bottle
c. 1933 - Grand Rapids,
USA
Ralmac Corp.
Smoothie - A-45
Cast aluminum
29 x 9 x 9

• Siphon bottle
1938 - Bloomfield, USA
Walter Kidde Sales Co.
Soda King Siphon
Norman Bel Geddes and
Worthen Paxton
Stainless steel, painted
cast aluminum, chromed
cast aluminum, chromed
steel and painted brass
25 x 12 x 12

• Shaker
c. 1935 - I
Sheet aluminum
15 x 9 x 9

• Siphon bottle
1941 - Saint Louis, USA
Sparklet Devices Inc./
Knapp Monarch
KM Charget
Dave Chapman
Copper-plated, painted
and chromed zamac
30 x 11 x 11

• Siphon bottle
1941 - Saint Louis, USA
Knapp Monarch
KM Charget
Dave Chapman
Stainless steel and painted
or chromed zamac
27 x 12 x 12

• Siphon bottle
c.1965 - CZ
Moravska Trebova
Painted cast aluminum
and polypropylene
26 x 19 x 10

• Siphon bottle
c.1936 - Bloomfield, USA
Kidde Mfg. Co.
5 - Soda King
Stainless steel, painted
zamac and cast aluminum
26 x 10 x 13

154-155

156-157

158-159

• Cocktail shaker
c. 1937 - New York, USA
Revere Copper and Brass
Inc.- Zephyr
W. Archibald Welden
Chromed brass
27 x 7,5 x 7,5

• Shaker
c. 1960 - USA
Irinware
Stainless steel
25 x 8,5 x 8,5

• Cocktail shaker
c. 1930 - USA?
Sheet aluminum
26 x 14 x 14

• Cooler cocktail shaker
c. 1950 - Syracuse, USA
Precision Castings Co.
Precision cooler
Painted, hammered
or polished cast aluminum
29 x 13 x 13

Whipped cream siphon
bottles

• c. 1955 - Paris, F
Auto-Siphon
Painted and polished cast
aluminum - 29 x 10 x 18

• 1961 - Paris, F
Société d'Application des
Gaz Liquéfiés - Fizacrem
Painted and polished cast
aluminum - 27 x 8 x 8

• c. 1960 - I
Cima
Stainless steel, chromed
steel, cast aluminum and
polypropylene - 21 x 14 x 14

• c. 1950 - Bloomfield, USA
Cream King Whipper - I
Polished cast aluminum,
painted zamac - 18 x 12 x 9

• c. 1955 - Milan, I
S.A.C.C.A.B - E.U.C.A
Cast aluminum with satin
finish
35 x 8,5 x 15 - 25 x 8,5 x 15

• Thermos bottle
1937 - Norwitch, USA
The American Thermos
Bottle Co. - "The
Hollywood Set" - 525F
Sheet aluminum with
satin finish, opaque glass
and bakelite
24,5 x 11 x 11

• Rotary-action cocktail
shaker
c. 1935 - USA
Polished sheet aluminum
and ethyl polymetacrylate
29 x 9 x 15

Shakers and siphons

Toasters

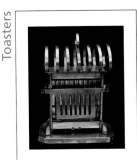

160-161

162-163

164-165

• **Thermos bottle**
c. 1938 - USA
Sears Roebuck & Co.
*Sheet aluminum
and polystyrene
27 x 10 x 10*

• **Thermos bottle**
c. 1950 - Eindhoven, NL
Philips
*Sheet aluminum
26 x 9 x 9*

• **Cocktail shaker**
c. 1935 - USA
*Sheet aluminum
27 x 11 x 11*

• **Toaster**
1915 - New Britain, USA
Landers, Frary & Clark/
Universal
*Nickel-plated steel,
nickel-plated brass, cast
iron and cardboard
25 x 18 x 10*

• **Toaster**
c. 1950 - D
Glem - M5
*Sheet, bakelite
and nickel-plated steel
25 x 19 x 19*

Toasters

• **c. 1937 - Ampere, USA**
Crocker-Wheeler Electric
Mfg. Co. - Toast-O-Lator - G
Alfredo De Mateis, Alvin
C. Goddard (technicians)
*Chromed steel, bakelite
and glass - 25 x 30 x 10*

• **1926 - Mineapolis, USA**
Waters Genter Co. -
The Toastmaster - 1-A-1
Charles P. Strite
(designer and technician)
*Chromed steel, chromed
brass, bakelite and rubber
19 x 26 x 12*

• **1947 - Philadelphia, USA**
Proctor Electric Co - 1481 A
Van Doren, Nowland
and Schladermundt
*Chromed steel, bakelite
and methyl polyacrylate
19 x 28 x 16*

• **c. 1939 - Niles, USA**
Calkins Appliance Co -
Breakfaster T2
*Polished cast aluminum,
unwrought cast aluminum,
sheet aluminum
and bakelite
12,5 x 28 x 20*

166-167

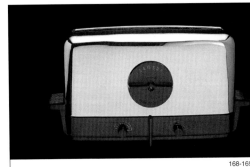

168-169

170-171

• **Toaster**
c. 1955 - D
Promotheus - WRS4
*Chromed brass,
bakelite and steel
28 x 20 x 16*

• **Toaster**
c. 1945 - Saint Louis, USA
The Toastwell Co. - 350
Joseph Pavelka Jr
and Victor Cornejo.
Paul Mc Cullough
(technician)
*Chromed steel
and bakelite
17 x 29 x 16*

• **Toaster**
1948 - Rochester, USA
Samson United Corp.
5147N
Harry L. Laylon
*Chromed steel
and bakelite
19 x 26 x 16*

• **Toaster**
c. 1960 - Bridgeport, USA
General Electric - 85T83
*Chromed steel and
bakelite
31 x 25 x 25*

• **Toaster**
c. 1938 - Buffalo, USA
Merit Made - Z
*Painted steel,
painted sheet aluminum
and bakelite
22 x 25 x 13*

Drinking | Eating

172-173

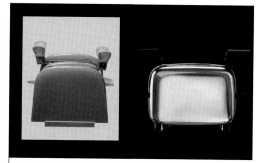

174-175

176-177

• Toaster
c. 1958 - Mansfield, USA
Westinghouse
Bakelite and chrome
18 x 25 x 14

• Toasters
1948 - Saint Mary Gray,
UK
Morphy-Richards - TA-1B
Chromed steel, bakelite
and sheet aluminum
18,5 x 29 x 15

• Toaster
c. 1956 - Milan, I
Neowatt B.C. - 84
Enamelled steel, nickel-
plated brass and melamine
20 x 21 x 12

• Toaster
c. 1962 - I
BJM
Chromed steel, nickel-
plated brass, bakelite
and sheet aluminum
29 x 22 x 19

• Toaster
c. 1960 - I
Electromeccanica Gaggia
Chromed steel
and bakelite-aluminum
23 x 42 x 20

178-179

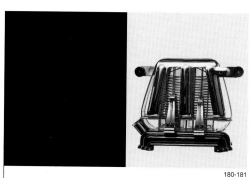
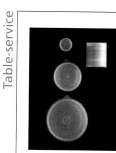

180-181

182-183

Toasters

• 1937 - Chicago, USA
Sunbeam - T-9
George T. Scharfenberg
Chromed steel and
bakelite - 19 x 26 x 14

• 1948 - Chicago, USA
Sunbeam - T20A
Robert D. Budlong and
Ivar Jepson.
Ludwig Koci (technician)
Chromed steel and
bakelite - 19 x 26 x 16

• 1938 - Elgin, USA
Mc Graw Elec. Co.
Toastmaster - 1B8

Victor Serota and Maurice
H. Graham (technicians)
Chromed steel and
bakelite - 16 x 26 x 14

• c. 1937 - New Britain,
USA
Landers, Frary & Clark/
Universal - FA 21-05
Chrome, bakelite - 20 x 22 x 12

• 1935 - Rochester, USA
Samson United Corp.
Tri-matic N°194
Abe O. Samuels. William
B. Connolly and Abe O.
Samuels (technicians)
Chromed and painted steel
and bakelite - 21 x 18 x 20

• Toaster
c. 1955 - H
Elekthermax - VP-3
Chromed brass,
bakelite and aluminum
17,5 x 22 x 11

• Coasters
n.d. - Orlando, USA
Tupperware - 566 - 567 -
568
High and low density
Polyethylene
8 x 8 x 9,5

• Bowls and lids
n.d. - Orlando, USA
Tupperware 154 - 155
Earl Silas Tupper
Low density polyethylene
3,5 x 12
4,5 x 17,5 x 16,5

• Small fruit dishes
c. 1950 - Orlando, USA
Tupperware - 754-27
Earl Silas Tupper
Low density polyethylene
6 x 10,5 x 10,5

Table sets

184-185

 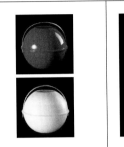 

186-187

188-189

• Tray - Salt shaker
and pepper shaker
c. 1950 - Orlando, USA
Tupperware - Dip-N-Serve
Earl Silas Tupper
Low density polyethylene
tray: diameter 36
salt shaker and pepper
shaker: 18 x 12 x 7

• Beakers
1947 - Orlando, USA
Tupperware
Earl Silas Tupper
Low density polyethylene
5,5 x 5 x 5

• Tea service
1946 - Orlando, USA
Tupperware
Millionaire Line
Earl Silas Tupper
Low density polyethylene
Plate: diameter 22
saucer: diameter 14
cup: 7 x 10 x 10

• Picnic set
c.1978 - Chicago, USA
Ingrid
High density polyethylene
and polystyrene
27 x 26 x 26

• Picnic set
c. 1980 - n.p.
High density polyethylene
and polystyrene
26 x 27 x 27

• Picnic service
c. 1978 - Hong Kong
Polystyrene and
polyethylene
20 x 25 x 25

190-191

 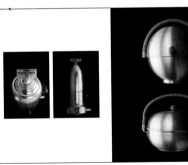 

192-193

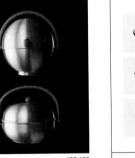

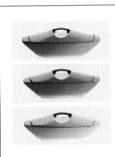 

194-195

• Set of tableware
1971 - Mettlach, D
Villeroy & Boch
Avant-Garde
Helen von Boch
Vitreous porcelain
27 x 26 x 26

• Egg cooker
c. 1950 - Chicago, USA
Sunbeam
Ivar Jepson
Polished cast aluminum,
sheet aluminum, bakelite,
polystyrene and chromed
steel - 20 x 19 x 13

• Bottle warmer
1950 - Chicago, USA
Sunbeam - B2
Ivar Jepson
Polished cast aluminum,
sheet aluminum, bakelite,
polystyrene and chromed
steel - 31,5 x 14 x 12,5

• Pastry warmer
1932 - New York, USA
Wright Accessories
Russel Wright
Brushed sheet aluminum,
rattan, wood - 25 x 25 x 24

• Steamer
1932 - New York, USA
Mirro
Russel Wright
Brushed sheet aluminum,
rattan, wood - 24 x 27 x 23

• Sauteuse pan
1959 - Fresnoy-le-Grand, F
Le Creuset - Sauteuse
Coquelle 3,5
CEI Raymond Loewy
Enamelled cast iron
11 x 32 x 21

• Sauteuse pan
1959 - Fresnoy-le-Grand, F
Le Creuset - Sauteuse
Coquelle 3,5
CEI Raymond Loewy
Enamelled cast iron
14 x 32 x 20,5

196-197

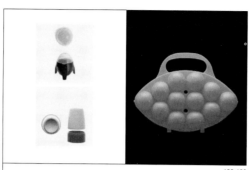

198-199

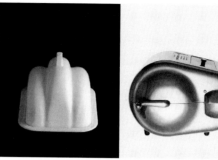

200-201

• **Turkey casserole dish**
c. 1936 - USA
Brand illegible
Sheet aluminum
18 x 47 x 29

• **Microwave egg cup**
1990 - E
De Galicia
High density polyethylene
10 x 8 x 8

• **Egg cup**
c. 1975 and c. 1960 -
Orlando, USA
Tupperware - 2166A-3 /
2167A-6 / 798-5 / 799-8
High density polyethylene
9 x 5,5 x 5,5

• **Egg box**
c. 1960 - F
Low density polyethylene
7 x 25 x 20

• **Butter dish**
c. 1950 - UK
Butter Dose
Polystyrene
8 x 10 x 13

• **Ice cream maker**
c. 1950 - Cleveland, USA
Freezer Inc. - Gardner Half
Minute Freezer
Polished cast aluminum
and methyl polyacrylate
19 x 22 x 25

202-203

204-205

206-207

• **Hard boiled egg stand**
c. 1946 - Paris, F
Surex
Bakelite
8 x 15 x 15

• **Egg cooker**
c. 1958 - Tokyo, JPN
Toshiba - BC-301
Yoshiharu Iwata
Painted steel, sheet
aluminum and bakelite
16 x 17 x 14

• **Potato cooker**
c. 1938 - Los Angeles,
USA
Na-Mac Product Corp.
Top-O-Stove
Polished cast aluminum
and steel
9 x 10 x 18

• **Meat fork**
c. 1960 - USA
Anonymous
Polished and engraved
cast aluminum
6 x 16 x 11,5

• **Automatic skillets**
1955 - New York, USA
Century Enterprise Inc.
Futuramic Automatic
Skillet Casserole - Sk 400
Morris Brandler
Sheet aluminum
and bakelite
19 x 33 x 36

Kitchen's Utensils

208-209

210-211

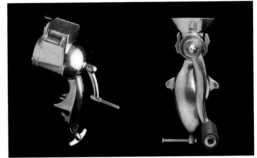

212-213

• Hot lunch box
c. 1945 - Oakland, USA
Privett Mfg. Co.
Thermette - 6 - Hot Lunch
Box Thermette
*Sheet aluminum, cast
aluminum and leather
25 x 27 x 13*

• Couscous maker
c. 1950 - Kewaskum, USA
Regal - 5223
*Sheet aluminum
and galvanised steel
32 x 26 x 25*

• Egg slicer
c. 1955 - D
Westmark Duplex Spezial
*Cast aluminum and steel
3,5 x 9 x 15*

• Egg slicer
1950 - UK
Egg Hygiene Slicer
*Melamine and steel
4,5 x 9 x 11,5*

• Egg cooker
c. 1950 - USA
*Polished cast aluminum
9 x 5,5 x 5,5*

• Cheesegrater
c. 1950 - CH
Zylyss
*Cast aluminum
31 x 11 x 22*

• Grinder
c. 1950 – Paris, F
Surm
*Polished cast aluminum,
steel and painted wood
28 x 11 x 23*

214-215

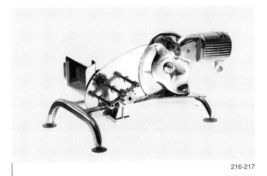

216-217

218-219

• Grinder
1949 - Philadelphia, USA
Enterprise
Herbert A. Wormeck
and Frederick P. Hess
*Chromed zamac, nickel-plated
cast iron and painted wood
18 x 27 x 25*

• Grinder
1950 - Kansas City, USA
Rival - Grind-O-Mat
Henry J. Talge
*Painted zamac, chromed
zamac, painted wood
and steel - 21 x 31 x 35*

• Grater
c. 1948 - Westfield, USA
Stanley Home Products

Salad maker n°512
*Painted cast aluminum,
steel, painted wood
24 x 24 x 26*

• Vegetable slicer
1950 - Kansas City, USA
Rival - Shred-O-Mat
Elton F. Whitfill and
Henry J. Talge
*Painted zamac, chromed
steel and painted wood
26 x 24 x 20*

• Tomato crusher
c.1980 – I
Master
*High density polyethylene
and steel - 30 x 30 x 17*

• Electric slicer
c. 1955 - Kansas City, USA
Rival - Electr-O-Matic
*Chromed zamac,
chromed steel, stainless
steel and rubber
20 x 44 x 25*

• Kitchen scale
c. 1968 - Annemasse, F
Terraillon
*ABS and polyacrylate
methyl
16 x 17 x 12*

• Kitchen scale
1971 - Annemasse, F
Terraillon - 2000
Marco Zanuso
*ABS and methylpoly-
acrylate
12 x 17 x 11*

• Kitchen scale
c. 1975 - Murrhardt, D

Soehnle
*ABS and methylpoly-
acrylate
8 x 21 x 21*

• Kitchen scale
c. 1975 - I
Prima - 3
*ABS
14 x 20 x 20*

• Kitchen scale
c. 1936 - USA
*Painted zamac
and painted steel
15 x 16 x 15*

Kitchen's Utensils

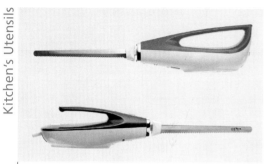

220-221

222-223

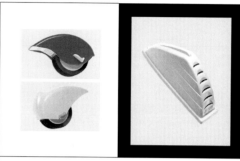

224-225

• Electric knife
1963 - F
SEB
Chapman, Goldsmith
and Yamasaki
ABS and stainless steel
10 x 48 x 6

• Electric knife
c. 1975 - F
SEB - Scovill - 516
ABS and stainless steel
9 x 47 x 6

• Hand crank knife
sharpener
1951 - Stockholm, S
A-B-Nils-Johan - Slip-Clara
Sheet aluminum
and bakelite
15 x 23 x 5,5

• Onion slicer
c. 1970 - I
E.R.O.
High density polyethylene
and stainless steel
8 x 7 x 15

• Onion slicer
1961 - D
Bébé Küchenboy
Polystyrene, cellulose
acetate and stainless steel
10 x 8 x 15

• Knife sharpener
c. 1940 - Perry, USA
Robeson Cutlery
Shure Edge
Cellulose acetate and steel
13,5 x 30 x 8

226-227

228-229

230-231

• Electric can opener
1957 - Grayslake, USA
Burgess Vibrocrafters Inc.
Douglas W. Anderson
Chromed zamac, chromed
steel, polystyrene - 9 x 20 x 20

• Can opener
1947 - Kansas City, USA
Rival - Can-O-Mat 45-S
Henry. J. Talge
Chromed zamac, cellulose
acetate - 8 x 20 x 9

• Can opener
1955 - Saint Louis, USA
Dazey - Canaramic 102

Joseph Palma Jr.
Chromed steel, chromed
zamac - 8 x 9 x 19

• Can opener
c. 1952 - New Kensington,
USA
Aluminum Cooking Utensil
Co. - Wear-Ever
Cast aluminum, cellulose
acetate - 8 x 18 x 10

• Can opener
1955 - Saint Louis, USA
Dazey - Canaramic 85
Joseph Palma Jr
Chromed steel, chromed
zamac - 7 x 12 x17

• Electric knife sharpener
1948 - Chicago, USA
Cory - DKS-2
Joseph Palma Jr and Palma
Knapp Associates
Cellulose acetate, bakelite,
steel and rubber
9,5 x 20 x 11

• Knife sharpener
1947 - Massachusetts,
USA
The Alden Spear's Sons Co.
Robo
Willis F. Thompson
Polystyrene, stone
and rubber
7,5 x 7,5 x 7,5

• Electric can opener
1957 - Milwaukee, USA
John Oster Mfg. Co. - 516
Alfred W. Madl
Painted zamac, chromed
steel and bakelite
23 x 26 x 22

234-235

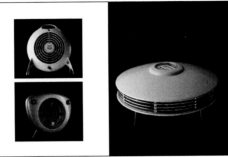

236-237

238-239

• Electric fan heater
c. 1958 - B
A.C.E.C - RS1
Painted zamac
30 x 26 x 14

• Electric heater
c. 1956 - UK
Sofono
Painted steel, chromed steel, sheet aluminum, cast aluminum and melamine
68 x 65 x 13

• Gas heater
1957 - F
Camping Gaz - Bidon Bleu - Cadet
Painted steel, sheet aluminum and brass
45 x 30 x 35

• Electric fan heater
c. 1960 - Aarau, CH
Schiesser & Luthy AG
Rex Therm
Painted steel, galvanised steel and polyethylene
34 x 37 x 11

• Electric fan heater
c. 1963 - B
Codumé - SF-7
Painted steel, chromed steel and polyethylene
18 x 35 x 35

• Electric heater
1937 - F
Saint-Gobain - Radiaver
1100 watts granité
René Coulon
Toughened, moulded glass, nickel-plated steel and aluminum
58 x 42 x 13

• Electric heater
c. 1940 - Chicago, USA
Wilkemp Industries - RH-3
Painted cast aluminum and sheet aluminum
75 x 21 x 20

240-241

242-243

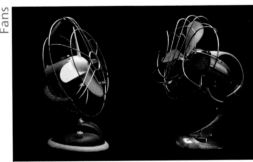

244-245

• Electric fan heater
c. 1945 - Chicago, USA
G-M Laboratories Inc.
Surf Season Air
Reticulated painted steel, galvanised steel, sheet aluminum and cast iron
37 x 29 x 21

• Electric fan heater
c. 1954 - F
M.S - Solair
Reticulated painted sheet aluminum, chromed steel, reticulated painted cast iron and bakelite
29 x 20 x 30

• Electric fan heater
1934 - Lyon, F
Calor - 662
Bakelite, sheet aluminum and chromed steel
36 x 36 x 14

• Electric heater
1945 - UK
The Gramophone Co Ltd.
H.M.V. - Lincoln F3
Christian Barman
Sheet aluminum, painted steel and bakelite
21 x 40 x 28

• Fan
c. 1951 - Milan, I
Marelli
Painted zamac, chromed brass, cast iron, high density polyethylene and elastomer
46 x 33 x 26

• Fan
c. 1938 - Torrington, USA
Fitzgerald - Standard
Attributed to Robert Heller
Zamac, nickel-plated zamac and nickel-plated steel
37 x 21 x 28

Heating | Cooling

246-247

248-249

250-251

- **Fan**
1955 - Eindhoven, NL
Philips - HA 2728
*Melamine, low density
polyethylene, polystyrene
and chromed brass
18 x 11 x 12*

- **Fan**
1955 - Eindhoven, NL
Radiola - RA 2726 –10
*Melamine, polystyrene,
polyethylene and
chromed brass
18 x 11 x 12*

- **Fan**
1955 - Eindhoven, NL
Radiola - RA 2627
*Melamine, low density
polyethylene, polystyrene
and chromed brass
18 x 11 x 12*

- **Ozone generator**
c. 1955 - F
*Cellulose acetate and brass
15 x 13 x 21*

- **Fan**
c. 1957 - Saint Paul, USA
B & B Remembrance –
Deskair
*Polystyrene and aluminum
9 x 20 x 19,5*

- **Fan**
1946 - Wichita, USA
Vornado - Vornadofan
12D1
Wayne Porter.
Ralph K. Odor and Kern
Dodge (technicians)
*Painted and unpainted
sheet aluminum,
steel and bakelite
57 x 55 x 33*

- **Fan**
c. 1956 - I
BJM - Kind
*High density polyethylene,
chromed steel
and elastomer
23 x 23 x 16*

- **Fan**
c. 1956 - F
*High and low density
polyethylene,
chromed steel
25 x 20 x 17*

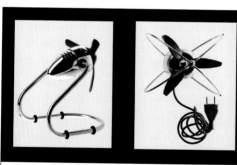

252-253

254-255

256-257

- **Fan**
1954 - Eindhoven, NL
Radiola - 514
*Chromed sheet
aluminum, chromed
steel and rubber
25 x 17 x 22*

- **Fan**
1953 - Milan, I
Fabbriche Ellettrotecniche
Riunite - Zerowatt - VE 505
Ezio Pirali
*Polished cast aluminum,
sheet aluminum,
chromed steel and rubber
18 x 14 x 25*

- **Fan**
c. 1933 - Elisabethport,
USA
DIEHL/Singer - Ribbonaire
Fredrik Ljunström
(designer and technician)
*Bakelite reinforced
with aluminum tube,
bakelite and fabric
32 x 11 x 18*

- **Fan**
c. 1955 - Turin, I
Aghetto
*Melamine, vinyl
and sheet aluminum
15 x 13 x 17,5*

- **Floor fan**
c. 1950 - Los Angeles, USA
Motionair Mfg. Co.
*Reticulated painted
cast aluminum, turned
cast aluminum, sheet
aluminum and steel
31 x 35 x 35*

- **Floor fan**
c. 1951 - Cincinnati, USA
W .W .Welch Co.
Air Flight Circulator
Raoul A. Lambert
*Bakelite, polystyrene,
aluminum and steel
35 x 38 x 38*

Vacuum cleaners

260-261

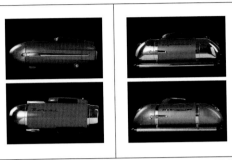

262-263

264-265

• Vacuum cleaner
c. 1955 - F
Tornado - Type T7
*Polished cast aluminum,
chromed steel
and polyamide
20 x 16 x 40 (motor only)*

• Vacuum cleaner
1939 - Chicago, USA
Kenmore - 167301
*Metallic painted steel
and sheet aluminum
27 x 23 x 65*

• Vacuum cleaner
c. 1946 - Cleveland, USA
Royal Vacuum Cleaner Co.
290
*Painted and chromed steel
25 x 19 x 60*

• Vacuum cleaner
c. 1950 - Rotterdam, NL
Holland Electro - XDM4
*Chromed steel, painted
steel and bakelite
25 x 19 x 60*

• Vacuum cleaner
c. 1950 - Rotterdam, NL
Holland Electro - Ultra -
Electric DM-8
*Chromed steel with
metallic paint finish
25 x 19 x 63*

• Vacuum cleaner
c. 1950 - Amsterdam, NL
Champion
Staubsauger
*Chromed steel and
steel with reticulated
paint finish
23 x 20 x 61*

• Vacuum cleaner
1937 - Old Greenwich, USA
Electrolux - XXX
Lurelle Guild
*Steel with imitation leather
coating, chromed steel
and cast aluminum
22 x 17 x 58*

• Vacuum cleaner
1939 - Stockholm, S
Electrolux - ZB 62 - Sixten
Sason
*Steel with PVC coating,
bakelite and aluminum
21 x 17 x 57*

• Vacuum cleaner
c. 1950 - New Britain, USA
Super Dynamic - B 6020
*Painted steel
25 x 28 x 58*

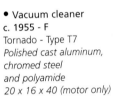

266-267

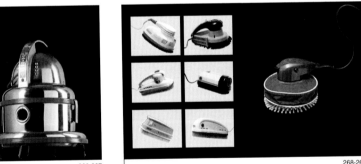

268-269

270-271

• Vacuum cleaner
1955 - Anaheim, USA
Interstate Engineering -
Compact C-5
Harold S. Ryden
*Reticulated and painted
cast aluminum,
chromed steel, PVC
30 x 24 x 48*

• Vacuum cleaner
c. 1948 - Welland, CAN
Fairfax Industries - CPD4
Harvey J. Mac Hallister
(technician)
*Chromed steel
and polyethylene
47 x 40 x 38*

Vacuum brushes

• 1956 - Milan, I
Lesa - Kleenette spalesina
Cellulose acetate - 10 x 10 x 18

• 1958 - Sochaux, F
Peugeot - Airbrosse
Polyamide - 11 x 13 x 19

• c. 1957 - Europe
Eldem
Melamine
11 x 7 x 20

• 1957 - Nice, F
Resistex - Bravo
*Melamine, bakelite
and rubber - 9 x 8 x 17*

• c. 1960 - F
Dyana
ABS - 10 x 8 x 19

• c. 1956 - I
Adler
Cellulose acetate - 10 x 9 x 20

• 1954 - Milan, I
Fratelli Chiminello - Elchim
Giuseppe De Goetzen
*Bakelite, cotton cloth and
polyamide - 11 x 14 x 12*

• Vacuum cleaner
c. 1938 - NL
Erres - SZ175
*Metallic painted steel,
bakelite and chromed steel
24 x 20 x 60*

Washing Cleansing

272-273

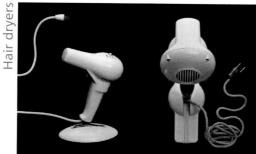

274-275

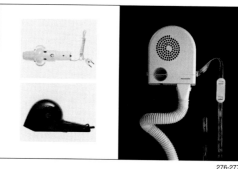

276-277

• Floor polisher
1932 - Stockholm, S
Electrolux - B 4
*Bakelite, polished cast
aluminum, chromed
steel and rubber*
25 x 32 x 28

• Floor polisher
1946 - Muskegon, USA
Clark Sanding Machine Co.
P12
De Witt Klausen
*Polished cast aluminum
and rubber*
23 x 30 x 30
(without handle)

• Hair dryer
c. 1940 - Racine, USA
Hamilton Beach -
Quick dry n°7
Painted zamac
23 x 9 x 22

• Hair dryer
1946 - UK
The Gramophone Co Ltd.
H.M.V. - HD-1
Christian Barman
*Painted bakelite,
bakelite, painted zamac
and painted steel*
30 x 22 x 13

• Hair dryer
1936 - Berlin, D
Siemens - Edir
Herbert Marloth
Melamine
21 x 9 x 7

• Hair dryer
c. 1960 - PL
Fema
Bakelite
25 x 13 x 7

• Hair dryer
c. 1980 - UK
Ronson - ES 001
ABS and PVC
22 x 18 x 6 (without tube)

278-279

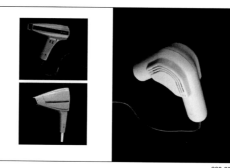

280-281

282-283

• Hair dryer
1944 - New Heaven, USA
The A. C. Gilbert Co.
Harry S. Preble, Jr
*Bakelite, chromed zamac,
painted zamac
and painted steel*
15 x 11 x 6
(without stand)

• Hair dryer
c. 1975 - Alençon, F
Moulinex - 55
Jean-Louis Barrault
*ABS and painted
aluminum*
19 x 21 x 8,5

• Hair dryer
c. 1970 - Lyon, F
Calor - 9204
High density polyethylene
23 x 20 x 7

• Hair dryer
c. 1980 - I
Sicer - 135
ABS
19 x 19 x 7

• Hair dryer
c. 1950 - Racine, USA
Racine Universal Motor
Corp. (Race) 65 - 9
*Chromed steel and
painted cast aluminum*
16 x 14 x 7

• Hair dryer
1948 - UK
GEC - DM 395
Melamine
21 x 17 x 8

• Hair dryer
1953 - F
Etoile - US-154
*Chromed brass, cellulose
acetate and chromed steel*
19 x 20 x 7

Hair dryers

284-285

286-287

288-289

• Hair dryer
c. 1965 - Alençon, F
Moulinex
Jean-Louis Barrault
Polystyrene and steel
16 x 11 x 20

• Hair dryer
c. 1965 - Alençon, F
Moulinex - ST1BV
Jean-Louis Barrault
Polystyrene and steel
21 x 11 x 30

• Hair dryer
c. 1956 - Lourdes, F
Elaul

Chromed steel, cellulose
acetate and polystyrene
22 x 13 x 23

• Hair dryer
1960 - F
Moulinex - 64 –
ABS and polystyrene
19 x 7 x 21

• Hair dryer
1927 - Lyon, F
Calor - 905
Chromed brass
and bakelite
25 x 24,5 x 12

• Hair dryer
c. 1988 - Lyon, F
Calor - 9241
ABS
9 x 9 x 9

• Hair dryer
c. 1936 - Sterling, USA
Wahl Clipper Corp.
G. Leo J. Wahl (technician)
Bakelite and aluminum
26 x 17 x 9

• Hair dryer
c. 1950 - UK
Forfex - John A. Frasen
Ltd.
Bakelite and nickel-plated
brass
21 x 27 x 10

Irons

290-291

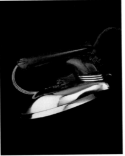

292-293

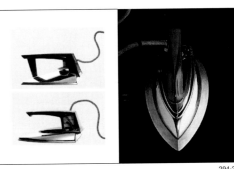

294-295

• Iron
c. 1960 - Lyon, F
Calor - 61
Jean Parthenay/Technès
Chromed steel, bakelite
and cast aluminum
10,5 x 13 x 13

• Iron
c. 1960 - I
Newman
Enamelled sheet steel,
bakelite, polystyrene
and cast aluminum
10 x 10 x 24

• Iron
c. 1950 - Liège, B
Nova
Chromed steel,
bakelite, melamine
and cast aluminum
12 x 12 x 24

• Iron
c. 1954 - F
Novex-Siebert - Ultramatic
Bakelite and chromed steel
11 x 10,5 x 23

• Iron
c. 1940 - Saint Louis, USA
Lady Dover
Chromed steel
and bakelite
13 x 11 x 23

• Iron
c. 1959 - Lyon, F
Calor - 51
Jean Parthenay/Technès
Chromed steel, bakelite
and cast aluminum
11 x 12 x 24

• Iron
c. 1945 - New Britain, USA
Landers, Frary & Clarck/
Universal - Strok-Sav-R
Chromed steel, bakelite
and cast aluminum
12 x 13 x 25

Irons

296-297

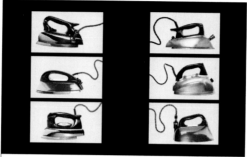

298-299

300-301

• Iron
1936 - UK
The Gramophone Co. Ltd.
H.M.V.
Christian Barman
*Enamelled steel, chromed
steel and bakelite
12 x 11 x 22*

Irons

•**1954 - Lyon, F**
Calor - Vapomatic N° 45
*Bakelite, chromed steel and
cast aluminum - 15 x 12,5 x 25*

• **c. 1960 - n.p.**
Techno Electra - Super Jet
Chrome, bakelite - 12 x 12,5 x 26

• **1953 - North Canton, USA**
Hoover
Russel Swann
*Chromed steel, bakelite and
cast aluminum -14 x 11 x 23*

• **1940 - Hartford, USA**
The Silex Co.
Judson Edwards
*Polished cast aluminum,
bakelite, brass - 14 x 11 x 26*

• **1953 - Paris, F**
Electro Jeannette - Vapofer
*Polished cast aluminum,
painted wood - 16 x 10 x 25*

• **c. 1940 - Saint Louis, USA**
Steem Electric Co. - Miss
Steem - 411
*Polished cast aluminum,
bakelite - 14 x 12 x 22*

• Iron
1941 - Sandusky, USA
Waverly Tool Co.
Petipoint
Clifford Brooks Stevens
and Edward P. Schreyer
*Chromed steel
and bakelite
13 x 12,5 x 26*

302-303

304-305

306-307

• Iron
c. 1960 - Genoa, I
Dandy - Super Dandy
*Bakelite and cast
aluminum
15 x 12 x 21*

• Iron
1946 - USA
General Mills - Tru-Heat 1B
+ Cm4A
Francesco Collura
and John Polivka
*Chromed steel, bakelite
and cast aluminum
14 x 12 x 32*

• Iron
1940 - Buffalo, USA
The Yale & Towne Mfg. Co.
Tip-Toe
*Bakelite, chromed steel
and cast aluminum
13 x 11x 25*

• Iron
1946 - Philadelphia, USA
Proctar
*Chromed steel,
polished cast aluminum
and bakelite
16 x 11 x 23*

• Iron
1939 - n.p.
Waverly Products Inc.
Team-O-Matic
Clifford Brooks Stevens
*Cast aluminum and wood
17 x 12 x 27*

• Irons **(1 - 2)**
1946 - USA
Saunders - Silver Streak -
1038
(1) *Toughened and
moulded painted glass,
chromed cast iron
and sheet aluminum
14,5 x 10 x 24*
(2) *Toughened and
moulded glass, chromed
cast iron and sheet
aluminum
14,5 x 10 x 24*

Irons

308-309

310-311

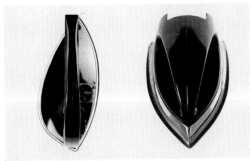

312-313

- Travel iron
c. 1950 - D
O & N - Mikro
*Melamine, chromed
cast iron, sheet
aluminum and bakelite
6 x 5 x 12*

- Travel iron
c. 1950 - Stockholm, S
Elektro-Gennel - Kronan
*Painted wood, cast
aluminum and steel
6,5 x 5 x 12*

- Travel iron
1946 - Coventry, UK
Lucas Holder - Smoothie
Lucas Holder
*Bakelite, aluminum
and chromed steel
6 x 4,8 x 11*

- Travel iron
c. 1950 - D
*Melamine, cast aluminum,
sheet aluminum
and bakelite
7 x 13 x 5*

- Iron
1947 - Saint Louis, USA
Knapp Monarch
Speed Iron
I. Huffman
*Bakelite, chromed steel
and polished cast
aluminum
13 x 13 x 22*

- Iron
1939 - Saint Louis, USA
Knapp Monarch
Flat Work Ironer
*Chromed steel
and bakelite
14 x 20 x19*

- Travel iron
1959 - Eindhoven, NL
Philips - 2380
*Chromed steel, bakelite
and cast aluminum
11 x 10 x 21*

- Travel iron
1956 - F
Noirot Kalorik
Voyage - 6011
*Bakelite and chromed steel
7 x 8 x 18*

Bathroom

314-315

316-317

318-319

- Electric vibrator
c. 1948 - USA
Andion - Magic Fingers
*Polished, painted and
reticulated cast aluminum,
chromed steel and rubber
coated steel
14 x 15 x 16*

- Vibrator
c. 1950 - Newark, USA
Spot Reducer Co. - "S"
*Sheet aluminum, rubber
and PVC
15 x 9 x 8*

- Vibrator
c. 1950 - New York, USA
Ward Green Co.
Redusaway
*Lacquered steel,
painted wood and
sheet aluminum
15 x 14 x 13*

- UV lamp
1951 - Eindhoven, NL
Philips - 2710
*Lacquered steel,
bakelite and glass
29 x 18 x 23*

- UV lamp
c. 1960 - Chicago, USA
Sun Kraft
*Brushed stainless steel
50 x 20 x 36*

Washing Cleansing

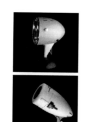

320-321

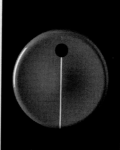

322-323

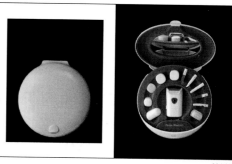

324-325

• UV lamp
c. 1954 - Hanau, CH
Solis - Soleil
*Painted sheet aluminum,
painted steel, melamine
and stainless steel*
32 x 18 x 21

• UV lamp
c. 1952 - Hanau, CH
Original Hanau
*Painted sheet aluminum,
bakelite, glass and steel*
27 x 15 x 26

• UV lamp
c. 1948 - Chicago, USA
Sun Kraft - Sun Kraft Jr
Frank Furedy (technician)
Chromed zamac
13 x 22 x 9 (when closed)

• Bathroom scale
c. 1983 - Annemasse, F
Terraillon
Christian de Poorter.
Crug Mairot, Jean P.
Aumard (techniciens)
ABS
5 x 28 x 33

• Bathroom scale
1974 - Annemasse, F
Terraillon
Marco Zanuso
ABS
9 x 33 x 33

• Beauty set
c. 1978 - Eindhoven, NL
Philips
ABS and polystyrene
4,5 x 24 x 25

326-327

328-329

330-331

• Massage instrument
c. 1960 - F
*Cellulose acetate
and wood*
4 x 14 x 8

• Electric curling tongs
c.1950 - Turin, I
Vielle
*Cast aluminum and
nickel-plated wrought iron*
11 x 9 x 30

• Vibrator
1953 - Glendale, USA
R.A. Fischer & Co.
Hollywood Vibra-Tone -
H-V 1700
Harry Raddon Greene.
Anna C. Fisher and Robert
Olivier Kubick (technicians)
Melamine and rubber
18 x 19 x 14

• Vibrator
1951 - Glendale, USA
R.A. Fischer & Co.
Hollywood Vibra -Tone -
H-V 1700

*Polished and painted
cast aluminum, polished
cast aluminum and rubber*
16 x 20 x 9

• Vibrator
c. 1956 - Hollywood, USA
The Relax-It Massage Co.
700
Casper J. Miller
(designer and technician)
*Chromed steel, bakelite,
rubber and painted
cast aluminum*
18 x 17 x 12

• Vibrator
1951 - Hollywood, USA
The Relax-It Massage Co.
700
Casper J. Miller
(designer and technician)
*Polished cast aluminum
and rubber*
17 x 19 x 9

Color separation
Galasele, Milano

Printed in Italy - October 2002
by Grafiche Milani, Segrate (Milano)
for 5 Continents Editions, Milano